Language
and Knowledge in the
Late Novels of
Henry James

Language
and Knowledge in the
Late Novels of
Henry James

Ruth Bernard Yeazell

The University of Chicago Press

Chicago and London

To My Parents

Ruth Bernard Yeazell has taught at Boston
University and now teaches English at the
University of California, Los Angeles,
where she is Associate Editor of
Nineteenth-Century Fiction. She is the author
of *The Death and Letters of Alice James,* as
well as several articles on British and
American fiction in scholarly journals.

The University of Chicago Press, Chicago 60637
The University of Chicago Press, Ltd., London

© 1976 by The University of Chicago
All rights reserved. Published 1976
Paperback edition 1980
Printed in the United States of America
86 85 84 83 82 81 80   98765432

Library of Congress Cataloging in Publication Data

Yeazell, Ruth Bernard
  Language and knowledge in the late novels
of Henry James.

  Includes index.
  1. James, Henry, 1843–1916—Style. I. Title.
PS2128.Y4   813'.4   75-46538
ISBN 0-226-95094-8
ISBN 0-226-95095-6 (paper)

Contents

Acknowledgments

Martin Price began this enterprise by introducing me to *The Golden Bowl* and continued as reader, critic, and friend over a period of several years; I find it hard to imagine the following pages without his invariably thoughtful advice and generous encouragement.

By reading an earlier version of this manuscript with her customary acuteness, Helen Vendler helped me to a genuine act of re-vision; her comments, suggestions, and example have proved invaluable.

I also want to thank Susan Snyder, from whom I first learned to read literature; David Cowden, who taught me to love novels; and Charles Feidelson, whose seminar on James opened to me new reaches of the novelist's imagination.

Finally, my greatest debt is to my husband, Stephen — now, as throughout the writing of this book, my best reader as well as my best friend.

Portions of the fourth chapter, "Talking in James," first appeared in *Criticism* (Wayne State University Press), vol. 16 (Spring 1974), and *PMLA* (Modern Language Association), vol. 91 (January 1976), and I am grateful to the publishers of these journals for permission to include them in somewhat altered form in this volume.

Except where otherwise noted, all references to the fiction of Henry James are to *The Novels and Tales of Henry James* (New York Edition), published by Charles Scribner's Sons (New York, 1907-9). Citations are followed by a series of four numbers: the first, in arabic numerals, is the volume number in the New York Edition; the next, in large roman numerals, the book number; the following, in small roman numerals, the chapter number; and the last, the page number, in arabic numerals preceded by "p." or "pp."

For the sake of convenience, all citations from James's Prefaces to the New York Edition have been taken from *The Art of the Novel* (*AN*), edited by R. P. Blackmur (1934; rpt. New York: Scribner's, 1962).

Knowledge,

knowledge, was a fascination

as well as a fear

(*The Golden Bowl*)

1   Translations into Late James

        Jamesian people and situations reappear with the soothing regularity of *topoi* in medieval romance. The New World innocent, baffled and betrayed by the moral ambiguities of the Old; the scheming lovers, too poor to marry one another, but not too scrupulous to prey on that innocence; the American millionaire, ready to purchase European culture, and the American Girl, eager to marry it — to the reader of *The American* or *The Portrait of a Lady*, the *données* of James's late novels should in theory seem reassuringly familiar. Yet a reader who begins *The Ambassadors* expecting to find another *American* is quite unlikely to feel reassured. For though Lambert Strether retraces Christopher Newman's journey to Paris, all imaginary Parisians do not apparently speak the same language. Citizens of one city, they nonetheless inhabit — as do Strether and Newman themselves — radically different fictional worlds.

Strether's Paris is not imaginatively contiguous with Newman's, nor is Maggie Verver's England with Isabel Archer's. Yet ironically, the experienced critic of James is in more danger than the naive reader of underestimating the distance from the one novelistic universe to the other. Bewildered and frustrated by the elaborate indirections of the late style, a reader confronting *The Wings of the Dove* for the first time scarcely needs reminding that he has before him a very different sort of thing from "Daisy Miller." But the Jamesian critic, accustomed to interpreting difficult fictions and rendering their language into his own, may have mastered this art of translation too well. He has made himself familiar with what "really" happens in the late novels: he knows that Madame de Vionnet is actually Chad's mistress, though Strether would like to believe she is not; that Milly Theale is literally dying, however unnamed her disease, and that Kate and Densher genuinely deceive her, however noble their talk; that Maggie Verver, at first blissfully ignorant, eventually discovers her sexual betrayal. Critics of any fiction, but especially of novels as elusive as these, necessarily begin with much that is unwritten plot summary and character sketch; the very act of intelligent reading demands that we implicitly summarize what is said and draw inferences from what, in late James at least, so often is not — that we postulate a consistent referential universe to which a novel's words finally point. But one thus translates James's late novels at the risk of doing violence to what is most idiosyncratic and exciting in them, of making their peculiarly fluid and unsettling reality something far more stable and conventional.[1] The distance at which critics must inevitably talk about novels is particularly dangerous here: the disquiet which we feel on first reading these novels should not be so easily assuaged.

To be true to that disquieting experience, we need to recover, if only temporarily, our fictional innocence — to remember just how disturbingly opaque even the most crucial of facts in James's late novels may seem. Sophisticated critical arguments over *The Golden Bowl*, for example, generally center on the comparative virtues of the novel's charming adulterers and of the dubiously innocent pair those adulterers betray.[2] But one ingenious critic, purporting to discuss the "ironic dimension" in James's fiction, manages to resolve such disputes simply by announcing that there is no adultery in *The Golden Bowl* after all: Charlotte and the Prince are not lovers, argues John Clair, but merely good friends who *pretend* to be lovers in order to awaken Maggie from her dangerous complacency.[3] Perversely naive as this solution may appear, we should not dismiss it too swiftly; if it suggests the willful blindness of the legendary subjects admiring the Emperor's new clothes, it has something of the small boy's refreshing truthfulness as well. For by prompting us to question closely how we do "know" that Charlotte and the Prince are lovers, it forces us to confront the deepest source of our own uncertainties—to acknowledge how epistemologically unsettling the actual experience of reading James's late fiction can be.

To preserve our sanity as readers we must of course resort to a kind of critical Occam's razor here, must assume that the mystery which Maggie so painfully uncovers is at least a genuine sexual betrayal and not the even more mysterious pretense of one. But that a late Jamesian novel should prompt such an overly ingenious reading should not be surprising. Our uneasiness about figures like Charlotte and the Prince goes deep—goes to the very nature of the fictional universe which James's late style creates. To allow that style fully to work on us is to find ourselves in a world where the boundaries between unconscious suspicion and certain knowledge, between pretense and reality, are continually shifting—a world in which the power of language to transform facts and even to create them seems matched only by the stubborn persistence of facts themselves. Necessary as we find it to determine what are finally truths here, what mere self-deceptions, and what lies, we do so only by distancing what actually happens to us as we read these novels—translating them in the process into safer and less exciting fictions.

If the hypothesis of the pretended affair seems more than a little absurd, it nonetheless remains true that few novels more strongly arouse our need to make such distinctions, to know conclusively the pretended from the real, than *The Golden Bowl*. Yet few novels more persistently elude our attempts to do so. At the heart of its moral situation are the elements of a familiar Jamesian melodrama: a man and woman, strongly attracted to one another but too poor, they feel, for marriage; their clandestine affair; and the innocent heiress who does marry the man, only to discover in the end the lovers' secret and the fact of her own betrayal. It is a story which James tells at least as early as *The Portrait of a Lady*; when the heiress's death is substituted for her marriage, it becomes the tale of *The Wings of the Dove* as well. As the treacherous women in this drama, Madame Merle, Kate Croy, and Charlotte Stant all share a striking family resemblance; so too do Isabel Archer, Milly Theale, and Maggie Verver as the unsuspecting victims. But the more closely we look at the later novels, the more these lines of fictional inheritance appear to shift and blur. Moral complexity, of course, is always a cardinal virtue of the Jamesian imagination: neither a Madame Merle nor a Charlotte Stant, for example, is ever the mere villainess of the piece. Yet even the nature of this moral complexity undergoes a curious transformation in the later novels. To compare the adulteress of *The Golden Bowl* with that of *The Portrait* is to recognize how powerfully the late style shapes our reading of human possibilities, and how strangely altered seem the premises of its fictional world.

As a characteristic Jamesian type, Charlotte Stant has far more in common with Serena Merle than a clandestine love affair, a lack of funds, and a distinct aversion to her native land. Though Charlotte is younger and presumably the less experienced, she shares with Madame Merle an exquisitely developed talent for the social life: "It had been established in the two households at an early stage and with the highest good humour that Charlotte was a, was *the*, 'social success' . . . (23, III, vi, p. 316). Like her prototype, who "does everything beautifully" (xviii, p. 153),[4] Charlotte is an accomplished piano player and a charming conversationalist, graced above all by "something about . . . [her] that carries things off" (23, II, iv, p. 184). Possessing neither family nor fortune, each woman manages nonetheless to parlay her immense charms into a continuous round of social engagements. Indeed, if Madame Merle is "the world itself" (xxiii, p. 220), in Ralph Touchett's ambiguous phrase, the Ververs, both more ingenuous and more dangerous than Ralph, bring Charlotte in "to do the 'worldly' for them" (23, III, vi, p. 318).

And "doing the worldly," for women such as these, is first of all an art of surfaces, of manipulating and controlling appearances. Madame Merle, in fact, has a "worship of appearances so intense" that it threatens to bore even that man of surfaces himself, Gilbert Osmond (li, p. 477). "One's self—for other people—is one's expression of one's self," she argues to the stubbornly romantic Isabel, "and one's house, one's furniture, one's clothes, the book one reads, the company one keeps—these things are all expressive" (xix, p. 175). As if bearing elegant witness to the truth of that argument, Charlotte Stant makes her triumphant entrance to the "great official party" in the third book of *The Golden Bowl*: having married Adam Verver and acquired house, furniture, and garments in abundance, she stands as magnificent evidence of "the *proved* private theory that materials to work with had been all she required and that there were none too precious for her to understand and use" (23, III, i, pp. 245–46). With "the unsurpassed diamonds that her head so happily carried, the other jewels, the other perfections of aspect and arrangement that made her personal scheme a success" (p. 246), the young Mrs. Verver enjoys powers of self-expression that her impecunious predecessor could only have envied.

Since fortune so often provides the measure of a Jamesian character's freedom, the question of comparative incomes is not a trivial one. But more than the size of their bank accounts divides the two women: what affects us most deeply is a matter of imaginative, not financial, resources. "I don't pretend to know what people are meant for," Madame Merle announces to Osmond as the former lovers plot Isabel Archer's fate, "I only know what I can do with them" (xxii, p. 210). It is a revealing admission—testifying not only to the purely instrumental limits of Madame Merle's knowledge but to the distance which separates the world of *The Portrait* from that of the later fiction. For the terms of the late novels allow of no such easy distinctions: in the language of a Charlotte Stant or a Kate Croy—in fact of virtually any character in the late James—knowing what to do with other people and "pretending to know what people are meant for" are most strangely mixed. Even characters ostensibly far less clever than Serena Merle have their "ideas": the late style grants to the humblest of its creatures the beginnings of a romantic imagination. And the more that acting and imagining thus merge, the more do characters in the late James seem to possess something of the artist's own power. Pretending to know what people are meant for—indeed not distinguishing between that pretense and what she wishes to do with her fellow creatures—a character like Charlotte Stant may become for the reader a disturbingly seductive force.

If we respond so differently to Madame Merle, it is not that she is a woman wholly lacking in imagination. On the contrary, in an indiscreet moment she reveals herself in dangerous possession of that faculty: "The idea did what so few things do," she tells Isabel after the scheme of marrying Pansy to Lord Warburton has collapsed—"it satisfied the imagination." "Your imagination, yes," Isabel retorts. "But not that of the persons concerned" (xlix, p. 452). As a mother who plots her daughter's future while carefully hiding the fact of her maternity even from that daughter herself, Madame Merle seems a woman who must live largely for such imaginative satisfactions. Yet despite this talk of pleasing her imagination, we can only wonder of Madame Merle here, as Isabel herself has earlier done, "what her relations might be with her own soul" (xix, p. 167). Whatever she might pretend her daughter and Warburton were meant for, whatever soothing visions she might entertain, such imaginings have for us no felt reality. All we know is that Madame Merle wanted the wealthy English lord to marry her child—thought she knew, once again, what she could do with other people.

However we finally judge a figure like Madame Merle,

her power over us is limited by the very way in which the novel grants her fictional being. When the Countess Gemini challenges her intentions toward Isabel, for example, the language of *The Portrait* keeps us safely at a distance from Madame Merle's inward response:

> "If I don't approve of your plan, you ought to know it in order to appreciate the danger of my interfering with it."
> Madame Merle looked as if she were ready to admit that there might be something in this; but in a moment she said quietly — "You think me more calculating than I am."
>
> (xxv, p. 234)

The narrator leaves us, like the poor Countess, to read Madame Merle from the outside: indeed this brief account of her reaction rests on the fiction that even the narrator himself has no direct access to Madame Merle's inner life. She is all a creature of surfaces here, and the effect is finally to intensify our sense of the empty evil within. That we have been privy to her conspiratorial talks with her former lover, as the Countess of course has not, only deepens the irony — makes us feel all the more strongly the disjunction between Madame Merle's cool disclaimers to Osmond's sister and the sinister facts of her plan. Though in verbal sophistication the Countess Gemini is no match for her partner here, her awkward bluntness ironically works in the end to confirm our darkest suspicions about Madame Merle.

But when Charlotte Stant confronts her own Countess Gemini in the person of Fanny Assingham, even our faculty for irony may grow severely strained. The apparent circumstances of the dialogue are remarkably similar: like Madame Merle in Osmond's garden, Charlotte has arrived at the diplomatic party with an unspoken "plan"; like the Countess Gemini, Fanny anxiously and rather ineffectually challenges that plan. Uneasy about Charlotte's intentions, guiltily aware of her own role in making the Ververs' marriages, Fanny worries over Maggie's conspicuous absence from the scene. That unworldly Princess has returned home with her father, but like Isabel lingering on the terrace with Osmond, she becomes here the unconscious center of a verbal duel. Yet to read this encounter in *The Golden Bowl* is to feel ourselves in a world whose laws resemble not those of Isabel's Florence but of Strether's Paris—a world in which, like those optical illusions whose figure and ground continually shift, "parts were not to be discriminated nor differences comfortably marked . . . . and what seemed all surface one moment seemed all depth the next" (*The Ambassadors*, 21, II, ii, p. 89).

That safe distance which divided us from Madame Merle has collapsed: we experience this confrontation as it is filtered through Charlotte's own consciousness. But it is not a mere difference in point of view that affects us so powerfully in this scene:

> He was always lonely at great parties, the dear Colonel —it wasn't in such places that the seed he sowed at home was ever reaped by him; but nobody could have seemed to mind it less, to brave it with more bronzed indifference; so markedly that he moved about less like one of the guests than like some quite presentable person in charge of the police arrangements or the electric light. To Mrs. Verver, as will be seen, he represented, with the perfect good faith of his apparent blankness, something definite enough; though her bravery was not thereby too blighted for her to feel herself calling him to witness that the only witchcraft her companion had used, within the few minutes, was that of attending Maggie, who had withdrawn from the scene, to her carriage. Notified at all events of Fanny's probable presence, Charlotte was for a while after this divided between the sense of it as a fact somehow to reckon with and deal with, which was a perception that made in its degree for the prudence, the pusillanimity of postponement, of avoidance—and a quite other feeling, an impatience that presently ended by prevailing, an eagerness, really, to *be* suspected, sounded, veritably arraigned, if only that she might have the bad moment over, if only that she might prove to herself, let alone to Mrs. Assingham also, that she could convert it to

good; if only in short to be "square," as they said, with
her question. For herself indeed particularly it wasn't a
question; but something in her bones told her that Fanny
would treat it as one, and there was truly nothing that
from this friend she wasn't bound in decency to take. She
might hand things back with every tender precaution,
with acknowledgements and assurances, but she owed it
to them in any case, and owed it to all Mrs. Assingham
had done for her, not to get rid of them without having
well unwrapped them and turned them over.

(23, III, i, pp. 249–50)

Though Jamesian tradition and the interests of simplicity
may require us to speak of Charlotte's "point of view" in such
a passage, the phrase has a comforting suggestion of psychic
consistency, even of single-mindedness, which is peculiarly
inappropriate here. For the language of this passage conveys
not a coherent viewpoint but a mind deeply and mysteriously in conflict with itself. Conscious pretense and innocent self-deception, fact and desire, the situation that
Charlotte knows to exist and the situation she wishes to
create—all merge in the elusive movements of James's prose.
And that prose shapes our response in ways of which even we
ourselves may be far from fully conscious.

We are allowed to come closer to Charlotte's psyche than
we ever do to Madame Merle's, but the result is not, as we
might expect, to confirm a sense of her hypocrisy, to
heighten an awareness of the discrepancies between Charlotte's public and private selves. We learn that Charlotte
half wants to avoid Fanny Assingham here, but her anxiety
does not frame itself, even privately, in terms of whether she
can successfully deceive that inquisitive friend. "You have
made me bad," Madame Merle may bluntly confess in a
moment alone with Osmond (xlix, p. 458), but the Charlotte who awaits Fanny in this scene is anxious to "prove to
herself, let alone to Mrs. Assingham also," that she can
"convert" her potentially bad moment to "good." For
Charlotte the desire to be " 'square' . . . with her question"
is not, it seems, a matter of satisfying appearances only, but

of a deeper need. Yet even as that need is articulated here, it is immediately negated: "For herself indeed particularly it wasn't a question; but something in her bones told her that Fanny would treat it as one." The hint of self-doubt implicit earlier disappears: Charlotte's wish to think well of herself has mysteriously become mental fact. By the close of the paragraph, Charlotte is busily anticipating her forthcoming "decency" to Mrs. Assingham; thinking not of avoiding her, but of how much she owes Fanny and how much she intends to give in return, Charlotte is already engaged in the mental process of converting all to "good." Unless we arbitrarily take these thoughts as self-conscious irony on her part — and there are no grounds for us to do so[5] — we must assume that, for the moment at least, her own anticipated decency has for Charlotte the force of psychic truth.

Though we have not yet witnessed the lovers' most compromising encounters, we may not of course feel wholly reassured; Charlotte's initial dread of Fanny, however quickly assuaged, must still leave us uneasy. And even her "decency" is itself characteristically ambiguous — a matter of "tender precaution," of "acknowledgements and assurances," not necessarily of genuine deeds. Yet it is through Charlotte's construction of things that we experience this scene, and the dizzying shifts of feeling here allow for no clear distinctions between self-deception and objective truth — grant us no fixed sense of a reality against which we are to measure and judge Charlotte's own. Indeed, the very fact that the passage begins with a sequence of perceptions whose truth we have no reason to doubt — an account of Colonel Bob ambiguously shared by Charlotte and the narrator himself — further serves to blur the line between private imaginings and narrative facts. Even a reader already familiar with the novel must find himself half surrendering to the power of Charlotte's inner language here, must feel his solid grasp of the "facts" temporarily give way before this creation of a reality so fluid and so potentially consoling.

And it is just such imaginative consolation which Charlotte offers to a worried Mrs. Assingham; the talk with Fanny is a fitting sequel to her implicit dialogue with herself:

> Maggie had come but to oblige her father — she had urged the two others to go without her; then she had yielded for the time to Mr. Verver's persuasion. But here, when they had, after the long wait in the carriage, fairly got in; here, once up the stairs and with the rooms before them, remorse had ended by seizing her: she had listened to no other remonstrance, and at present therefore, as Charlotte put it, the two were doubtless making together a little party at home. But it was all right — so Charlotte also put it: there was nothing in the world they liked better than these snatched felicities, little parties, long talks, with "I'll come to you tomorrow," and "No, I'll come to *you*," make-believe renewals of their old life. They were fairly at times, the dear things, like children playing at paying visits, playing at "Mr. Thompson and Mrs. Fane," each hoping that the other would really stay to tea. Charlotte was sure she should find Maggie there on getting home — a remark in which Mrs. Verver's immediate response to her friend's enquiry had culminated. She had thus on the spot the sense of having given her plenty to think about, and that moreover of liking to see it even better than she had expected. She had plenty to think about herself, and there was already something in Fanny that made it seem still more.
>
> (23, III, i, pp. 252-53)

Challenged to account for Maggie's absence, Charlotte responds with this reassuring tale of "snatched felicities" and childlike games at teatime — a tale all the more soothing because it grants to the Ververs too their imaginative consolations. It is a charming instance of Charlotte's pretending to know just what others are meant for. Yet even to speak of her "pretending" here is artificially to distance and moralize the text, to seek refuge in the distinctions of another, more epistemologically stable world. Madame

Merle's clear terms no longer hold: if Charlotte's vision of the fictive Mr. Thompson and Mrs. Fane is an elaborate invention, it is not quite — so far as we can know here — mere pretense. We may be left, as is Fanny herself, with a vague sense of disquiet, but for all its cloying sweetness, this little narrative has a peculiar force. Like so much late Jamesian dialogue, Charlotte's way of "putting it" is more than a manner of speaking: it is also a way of imagining, indeed of creating the terms of her world.

For the reader to refer to a fictional character in this fashion is admittedly very odd: it is Henry James, after all, and not Charlotte Stant who has imagined the world of *The Golden Bowl*, even as it is Henry James whose characteristic syntax and metaphors are finally under consideration here, not Strether's or Milly Theale's or Kate Croy's. But if this elementary distinction often seems blurred in the pages that follow, it is at least intentionally done. For however we may try to keep the minds of the narrator and his characters properly distinct, the language of the late novels themselves continually defeats us. Occasionally the narrator does intrude *in propria persona*;[6] occasionally he attributes a mental phrase or image quite explicitly to one of his characters, but far more characteristic is that ambiguous blurring of voices noted earlier — the way in which "dear" Colonel Assingham seems to take shape at once in the narrator's words and in Charlotte's own. Of course in part this is simply a convention of third-person narrative, to be accepted like any other: in *le style indirect libre*, as it is often known, we move imperceptibly from the narrator's account of his character's thoughts to intimations of that character's own inner language — what we take to be, at least, his private mental diction and syntax.[7] But this fluidity affects us all the more strongly in the late novels because of the consistent stylization of James's language — those striking idiosyncrasies of cadence and diction that enable us to recognize virtually any passage, whatever its subject or ostensible source, as unmistakably Jamesian. When even the likes of Susan Stringham, that loyal daughter of Burlington, Vermont, may think and speak in such cadences, the boundaries between the minds of narrator and characters seem fluid indeed.

Like so much in the late fiction, these shifting boundaries may leave the reader rather uneasy — may prompt him, if he is a critic, to attempt to translate the late James into the idiom of other, more comfortable fictions. "The locus of the image will indicate responsibility for the creation of meaning," one such critic reasonably asserts, as he tries to determine which images must therefore belong to the narrator and which to his characters — granting Maggie Verver, for example, the image of the coach with the missing wheel (24, IV, ii, pp. 23-24), but allotting the pagoda (24, IV, i, pp. 3-6) to the narrator, on the theory that it is too complex and exotic a metaphor for the Princess's newly awakened imagination.[8] But in our actual reading of the novels, "responsibility for the creation of meaning" rarely seems so clearly fixed: if one passage suggests that the oriental pagoda fantasy is the narrator's, not Maggie's, in another the distinction seems simply to have dissolved. Teasing us with the suggestion that people may possess, artist-like, the power to make the terms of their world, the late style defies our attempts to impose a more conventional logic, appeals instead to deeper and less rational needs.[9]

It is not merely the extenuating circumstances of her case that draw us to a character like Charlotte Stant, then; what we respond to more immediately — if also perhaps more amorally — is something we can only call, as Maggie herself does, Charlotte's "great imagination" (23, II, iv, pp. 181-82). And no later knowledge of the facts behind *The Golden Bowl* — of the adultery itself, of Maggie's awakening and her pain, even of Charlotte's own eventual suffering — can wholly alter that response. To approach the late James as if his language were a beautiful and mysterious screen placed between us and the moral facts of the novels is to miss more than half his power: in few novels do the realities of moral life seem so compelling, yet for few novels do social and ethical categories feel so incomplete, even so removed from what actually happens to us as we read. For whatever the moral judgments with which we end, a language which moves so fluidly between fact and desire, between the truth of outer circumstance and the truth of inner need, offers us, from moment to moment, consolations all its own.

In a late and unusual excursion into metaphysics, James tentatively speculated on the possibility of survival after death — approaching it, characteristically, through the satisfactions of the conscious life:

> What had happened, in short, was that all the while I had
> been practically, though however dimly, trying to take
> the measure of my consciousness. . . . I had learned, as I
> may say, to live in it more. . . . I had doubtless taken thus
> to increased living in it by reaction against so grossly
> finite a world — for it at least *contained* the world, and
> could handle and criticise it, could play with it and deride
> it, it had *that* superiority: which meant, all the while,
> such successful living that the abode itself grew more and
> more interesting to me, and with this beautiful sign of its
> character that the more and the more one asked of it the
> more and the more it appeared to give.[10]

Consciousness here offers a means of "containment" if not of transcendence: like one of his own fictional characters, James seeks to escape by its means the limits of "so grossly finite a world." Yet in his last novels, at least, that world still makes itself very much felt — indeed finally exerts its pressures all the more strongly because it is so often evaded and suppressed. It is, after all, from "so grossly finite a world" that the traditional stuff of novels, unlike romances, is made. And it is ultimately with the finite and the gross that we identify reality here as well. Despite the romantic imaginations of Charlotte and some of her critics, the cruel effects of the adultery in *The Golden Bowl* are finally all too unmistakable: when the Princess awakens to knowledge in the second half of the novel, she encounters what we can only assume is the painfully real.

Of course even to talk about knowledge, as succeeding chapters will continually do, is to take for granted that there are finally facts in these novels to be known — facts which we sense, however they may go unnamed, and facts which the characters themselves must eventually confront. For reader and character alike, these "things we cannot possibly *not* know, sooner or later, one way or another" (Preface to *The American, AN*, p. 31) exert tremendous power: unconscious evasions and conscious lies give way, inexorably, to the fascinations of knowledge. And subsequent chapters will explore the style of that surrender. But if the novelistic facts so discounted in the above discussion appear substantially to reassert themselves in the following pages, uncovering those facts is not the reader's only stylistic pleasure. For the peculiar excitement of reading the late James derives not only from the melodramatic facts so gradually disclosed but from the imaginative needs with which they are continually at war — the needs of consciousness to "handle, criticise, play with, deride," the need to escape from and even to transform "so grossly finite a world." It is from the tension between those needs and the hidden limits the world imposes that the deepest emotional energies of James's late fiction come. Only by acknowledging the power of each can we be true to the strange pleasures which reading the late James provides.

2   The Syntax of Knowing

The men and women in Henry James's late novels seem never to take to their beds—except, like Milly Theale, to die. Sleep rarely overcomes them: only at the very beginning of *The Ambassadors*—when the alternative is a long discussion with Waymarsh—does Strether express an active interest in "put[ting] in eight hours" (21, I, ii, p. 31). Even more remarkable for people who live so intensely in the mind, James's characters scarcely ever dream.[1] Creatures of an age which produced Freud, they nonetheless strenuously resist any surrender to the unconscious. Less than twenty years before Molly Bloom drifts leisurely and volubly to sleep, Maggie Verver knows "there was no question for her ... of closing her eyes and getting away ..." (24, V, ii, p. 232).

The more deeply moving his recent experience, the more energetically does the Jamesian character struggle to keep awake. Sleepless meditation begins as early as Isabel's fireside vigil in *The Portrait of a Lady* (xlii), but it is in the novels of the major phase that the need for wakefulness is most unrelenting. After his painful discovery of Chad and Marie de Vionnet, floating down the river in an intimacy he suddenly finds all too obvious, Strether "scarce ... [goes] to bed till morning" (22, XI, iv, p. 262). Milly Theale's deathbed letter, presumably bearing her last words and her legacy to Densher, arrives at that young man's lodgings on Christmas eve and makes for a night "mercilessly wakeful" (20, X, iii, p. 351); Densher relinquishes his vigil only "with the arrival of the Christmas dawn ... late and grey" (p. 352)—though Milly's letter still remains unopened. Maggie Verver cannot afford even "to snatch forty winks" while her companions play bridge (24, V, ii, p. 231), and for her too "there came at last a high dim August dawn when she couldn't sleep ..." (24, V, iv, p. 293)—a sunrise which offers more light, but no more sleep, than Densher's Christmas dawn. The discovery of her future husband's intended bigamy moves Charlotte Brontë's Jane to a strange and terrible dream;[2] the discovery of her husband's actual adultery prompts Maggie Verver to ever more furious thought. In James's late novels, a crisis demands tireless speculation: apparently it is not only a shrinking from sexual passion—a timidity of which they have often been accused—that keeps Jamesian characters away from their beds.

All this intense wakefulness betokens a world in which the deepest reaches of the psyche—at least as the twentieth century understands them—rarely come into view. To a modern reader, long accustomed to the idea that much of consciousness operates below the level of language, the very look of a Jamesian meditation on the page suggests a mind in which the intellect is very much in control. For the unconscious does not, we suspect, obey the rules of grammar and of syntax, and James's men and women think in sentences which no more resemble the unpunctuated flow of words in Molly Bloom's final monologue or the bizarre strings of neologisms in *Finnegans Wake* than their sleeping habits resemble those of Joyce's rather drowsy characters. Though the Jamesian sentence strains, it does not break: no stream of consciousness, the critics all agree, flows through the pages of James's late fiction.[3] To readers raised on Joyce, Woolf, and Faulkner, James's late style seems firmly committed to the world of the waking intellect. The novels of the major phase "are strictly novels of intelligence rather than of full consciousness," wrote F. O. Matthiessen. James's characters appear to live "off the top of their heads"[4]—heads, Matthiessen might have added, recalling that of the Master himself in Max Beerbohm's famous caricatures: huge, swollen, and immensely top-heavy.

But if the heads of James's characters seem top-heavy,

that is only because those heads are swollen under vast pressures from below. For in the minds of James's men and women the force of all that is unconscious and unspoken makes itself continuously and powerfully felt. James's late novels do not finally give us intelligence *rather* than full consciousness: what the late style dramatizes is the painful struggle of the intelligence literally to come to terms *with* full consciousness—and thus in some measure to hold it in check. "Terms" are of course the intellect's own province: the intellect does retain control, but that control is much more precarious—and more hard-won—than might at first appear. For James's heroes and heroines, to stay awake and alert is thus imperative, especially at moments of crisis, for to relax into sleep is to risk a loss of control and to allow suppressed feeling and knowledge irresistibly to surface.

Toward the end of James's last completed novel, *The Golden Bowl*, comes a moment when its heroine, Maggie Verver, hovers extraordinarily close to the brink of surrender. The danger arises, as for Maggie it always threatens to, out of her deep passion for her own husband, the Prince. She and Amerigo have had their first intimate talk since their confrontation over the shattered golden bowl: having denounced Charlotte as "stupid" and proclaimed his own "good faith" (24, VI, ii, pp. 348–50), the Prince begs from his wife "still one thing more." "I'll do anything, if you'll tell me what," she responds. "Then wait," he says—and he repeats the word twice—"Wait. . . . Till we're really alone." The entire scene is filled with the promise of their imminent reunion, and as she turns to go, her hand on the knob of the door, Maggie suddenly finds herself paralyzed by the strength of her desire—"almost with a terror of her endless power of surrender":

> The sensation was for the few seconds extraordinary; her weakness, her desire, so long as she was yet not saving herself, flowered in her face like a light or a darkness. She sought for some word that would cover this up. . . .

> She had, with her hand still on the knob, her back
> against the door, so that her retreat under his approach
> must be less than a step, and yet she couldn't for her life
> with the other hand have pushed him away. He was so
> near now that she could touch him, taste him, smell him,
> kiss him, hold him; he almost pressed upon her, and the
> warmth of his face — frowning, smiling, she mightn't
> know which; only beautiful and strange — was bent upon
> her with the largeness with which objects loom in dreams.
> She closed her eyes to it, and so the next instant, against
> her purpose, had put out her hand, which had met his
> own and which he held. Then it was that from behind her
> closed eyes the right word came. "Wait!" It was the
> word of his own distress and entreaty, the word for both
> of them, all they had left, their plank now on the great
> sea. Their hands were locked, and thus she said it again.
> "Wait. Wait." She kept her eyes shut, but her hand, she
> knew, helped her meaning — which after a minute she was
> aware his own had absorbed. He let her go — he turned
> away with this message, and when she saw him again his
> back was presented, as he had left her, and his face staring
> out of the window. She had saved herself and she got off.
>
> (24, VI, ii, pp. 352–53)

As the Prince draws near, sense impressions crowd in upon
the Princess with a speed and intensity we might more readily
associate with the hedonistic Molly Bloom than with James's
heroines: ". . . she could touch him, taste him, smell him,
kiss him, hold him." Significantly, her husband seems to
Maggie like a figure in a dream — immensely attractive, yet
"looming" before her with a rather nightmarish pressure.
Yielding to that dream is at once appealing and terrifying,
for sexual surrender becomes identical here with the loss of all
conscious control. The moment recalls a similar one at the
close of *The Portrait of a Lady* — Caspar Goodwood's kiss
"like a flash of lightning" and Isabel's terrified flight (lv, p.
519) — but the sexual tension in the later scene goes deeper
still: [5] though Isabel finds herself momentarily tempted to

"sink and sink" in Goodwood's arms, the force of Maggie's desire for her husband is matched only by her terror of succumbing to that desire.

The closer the Prince looms, the more vague and enigmatic becomes the language which records her perceptions: her desire shows in her face "like a light or a darkness"; the Prince's face is "frowning, smiling, she mightn't know which." With the loss of control comes a blurring of verbal distinctions. In her terror, then, Maggie searches for "some word that would cover this up" — and it is with a word that she finally saves herself: "Wait," she says, echoing Amerigo's own last word to her. Repeating it, she appeals to a bond between them, creates for husband and wife a common language ("It was the word of his own distress and entreaty, the word for both of them"). And the word of course postpones their mutual surrender: it is a "plank" to which she can cling, lest the formless "sea" of passion overwhelm her. With language — "the right word" — the conscious self resists and controls the psyche's unspoken and only half-conscious demands. Maggie Verver's "Wait" is a far cry from Molly Bloom's "Yes."

In its avoidance of direct sexual surrender, the moment is of course characteristically Jamesian: even when Kate Croy visits Densher's Venetian rooms in *The Wings of the Dove* — paying with her sexual compliance for Densher's continued participation in their plot — James carefully veils the actual encounter from our view. But the sexual reticence of his late fiction is in direct proportion to the felt presence of sexuality as a force at the very center of human life. Beginning with the fiction of the late nineties — *What Maisie Knew, The Turn of the Screw, The Awkward Age* — and continuing through *The Sacred Fount* and the novels of the major phase, sexual passion becomes the central mystery, the hidden knowledge which the Jamesian innocent must at last confront. Maggie is terrified of Amerigo's approach precisely because she senses her own "endless power of surrender": this scene between the Princess and the Prince reveals most dramatically that in shrinking from sexual encounter she responds to the intensity of her own desire.

Somewhat earlier in *The Golden Bowl*, as she struggles to face the whole truth about the Prince's relations with Charlotte, Maggie finds herself thinking, "Knowledge, knowledge, was a fascination as well as a fear . . ." (24, IV, viii, p. 140). Though the knowledge in question most directly concerns the facts of her husband's adultery, it is knowledge in a deeper sense as well—even, perhaps most especially, sexual knowledge. What James's characters suppress and evade—the dreams, the sexual desire, the awareness of their own evil—lies, paradoxically, very close to the surface of their minds. Full consciousness is at once "a fascination" and "a fear." And it is the recording of the mind's effort to walk the tightrope between that fascination and that fear which makes James's late style at once so elusive, so "difficult," and so exciting.[6]

When Maggie Verver begs her husband to "wait," she asks that he perform in a typically Jamesian fashion. James's men and women often seek refuge in postponement and delay: Maggie by putting off reunion with the Prince; Densher and Kate by delaying their marriage and awaiting Milly's death; Strether by postponing his return voyage to America. From the very first moment at which Strether lands at Liverpool, in fact, *The Ambassadors* becomes one long delaying action: "The same secret principle . . . that had prompted Strether not absolutely to desire Waymarsh's presence at the dock, that had led him thus to postpone for a few hours his enjoyment of it, now operated to make him feel he could still wait without disappointment" (21, I, i, p. 3). The anxious Strether who glances repeatedly at his watch on his first walk around Chester with Miss Gostrey discovers in Paris the delights of procrastination—putting off from day to day the completion of his mission and a final confrontation with Mrs. Newsome. But Strether procrastinates in a deeper sense as well: for as long as he is able, he avoids any conscious knowledge of the affair between Chad and Madame de

Vionnet. To face that knowledge is for Strether far more terrible than to face the awe-inspiring Mrs. Newsome. Postponing conscious recognition, he remains—at least temporarily—safe: safe as Densher is, anxiously suppressing full awareness of the plot against Milly; safe as Milly herself, struggling to avoid the certain knowledge of her own death; safe even as Maggie at the beginning of *The Golden Bowl*, unconsciously prolonging her dream of innocence. Though we ourselves may not be fully conscious of the fact, to follow the language in which James's characters think is to sense beneath the surface the intensity of their passion for delay. For it is in the very shape and form of the Jamesian sentence that the terror of full consciousness most makes itself felt.

But even Strether, that arch-procrastinator, must finally confront the facts he has so long evaded:

> He was rather glad, none the less, that they had in point of fact not parted at the Cheval Blanc, that he hadn't been reduced to giving them his blessing for an idyllic retreat down the river. He had had in the actual case to make-believe more than he liked, but this was nothing, it struck him, to what the other event would have required. Could he, literally, quite have faced the other event? Would he have been capable of making the best of it with them? This was what he was trying to do now; but with the advantage of his being able to give more time to it a good deal counteracted by his sense of what, over and above the central fact itself, he had to swallow. It was the quantity of make-believe involved and so vividly exemplified that most disagreed with his spiritual stomach. He moved, however, from the consideration of that quantity—to say nothing of the consciousness of that organ—back to the other feature of the show, the deep, deep truth of the intimacy revealed. That was what, in his vain vigil, he oftenest reverted to: intimacy, at such a point, was *like* that—and what in the world else would one have wished it to be like? It was all very well for him to feel the pity of its being so much like lying; he almost blushed, in the dark, for the way he had dressed the possibility in vagueness, as a little girl might have dressed her doll. He had made them—and by no fault

of their own—momentarily pull it for him, the possibility, out of this vagueness; and must he not therefore take it now as they had had simply, with whatever thin attenuations, to give it to him? The very question, it may be added, made him feel lonely and cold. There was the element of the awkward all round, but Chad and Madame de Vionnet had at least the comfort that they could talk it over together. With whom could *he* talk of such things?—unless indeed always, at almost any stage, with Maria? He foresaw that Miss Gostrey would come again into requisition on the morrow; though it wasn't to be denied that he was already a little afraid of her "What on earth—that's what I want to know now—had you then supposed?" He recognised at last that he had really been trying all along to suppose nothing. Verily, verily, his labour had been lost. He found himself supposing innumerable and wonderful things.

(22, XI, iv, pp. 265–66)

The impatient reader might well want to echo Maria Gostrey's imaginary question: what on earth, after all, *has* Strether been supposing? The point of course is that he has been struggling desperately "to suppose nothing"—to think about Chad and Marie in terms so vague and evasive as to preserve both their innocence and his own.

Drifting in their boat together, pink parasol and all, the lovers have made even for Strether a fact too palpable to ignore; his country idyll shattered, the man from Woollett is at last face to face with "the intimacy revealed." The passage quoted above marks the climax of his revelation: by its conclusion "innumerable and wonderful things" have rushed to fill Strether's anxiously guarded mental vacuum. Having "dressed" so much in "vagueness," he now confronts the truth in an acute state of shock—a shock which is all the more powerful because Strether must recognize that by his very vagueness he has conspired in his own deception. Yet even at this extreme moment of revelation Strether's thoughts move by postponement and indirection: poor Strether is at once propelled toward discovery and in terrified flight from it. For the closer the Jamesian character comes toward hidden truths, the more intensely he is fascinated by them, the stronger grows his fear as well. Looking closely at the language of Strether's mind, we hear him too calling "Wait!"—though it is only a subconscious voice which speaks, and there is no one to listen but Strether himself.

Compelled at last to acknowledge that Chad and Marie are lovers, Strether nonetheless keeps the terms of recognition remarkably vague: at his most explicit, he thinks of their liaison as "intimacy." Where he once supposed "nothing," he now supposes "innumerable and wonderful things" (or, as all editions but the New York have it, "everything").[7] Our imaginations may make those "things" concrete, but Strether's prudently refrains. "Intimacy," he thinks, "was *like* that," but even as the stress he mentally imparts conveys the force of his sudden recognition, we may well find ourselves wondering exactly what intimacy—Chad's and Marie's in particular—*is* like. "That" is a vague quality indeed, and like so many of the pronouns in which Strether's conscious mind takes refuge, its antecedent proves rather elusive. Intensely aware of "the deep, deep truth of the intimacy revealed," the man from Woollett still struggles to hold the concrete noun—and thus the disturbing facts—at a safe distance. And even as Strether has lingered so long in Paris, postponing all final confrontations, so too does his mental syntax characteristically hesitate and delay.[8] Strether's thought does not move in simple sequences of noun-verb-object any more than his person moves with rapidity and decision to carry out Mrs. Newsome's errand. "He had made them—and by no fault of their own—momentarily pull it for him, the possibility, out of this vagueness . . .": "vagueness" has presumably been left behind, yet Strether's mind pauses, qualifies, postpones—lingering even now partially to absolve the lovers from blame. Beneath Strether's mental syntax we sense that part of himself which still wishes to avoid direct conclusions, to delay the involuntary push of full consciousness. It is the same impulse which moves him, even at this late date, to shrink back from the immediacy

of names, to think not of illicit sex, but of "it," "the possibility."

But for one who has managed for so long to suppose
"nothing," Strether uncovers the truth with rather little,
after all, in the way of new concrete evidence. Seeing the
unknown man and woman in their boat, "expert, familiar,
frequent" (22, XI, iv, p. 256); recognizing them the next
moment as Chad and Marie, curiously anxious to avoid a
meeting, Strether suddenly finds the pieces fall irresistibly
into place. If all at once his discovery seems inevitable, it is
not that the facts are now so glaringly obvious—or that they
were so obscure before—but that by this time Strether is
ready to awaken at even the slightest touch. "It was a sharp
fantastic crisis that had popped up as if in a dream . . ."
(pp. 257-58)—"popped up" as if from a part of Strether
which has known all along that some such disaster was to
come. In the scene by the river Strether unexpectedly meets
not only his vacationing friends but his own worst fears. It is
a recognition scene with a vengeance.[9]

For like so many of the characters in James's late novels,
Strether has long been in the uncomfortable position of
sensing more than he can allow himself to know. After the
confrontation by the river he still resists full consciousness,
but his struggle is painful precisely because the battle was in
one sense lost even before it was joined: Strether already
knows what he deeply fears knowing. His indirections and
evasions may threaten our patience, but we feel at the same
time a powerful excitement—an excitement which stems in
large part from the tension between Strether's resistance and
the almost inexorable coming of the recognition he fears.
For the very rhythms of James's late style enact this relentless
unfolding of awareness; in the language itself we sense the
peculiar force with which knowledge—half-dreaded, half-
desired—thrusts itself upon the conscious mind.

Few characters in the late James feel this sense of inner
pressure so strongly as does Maggie Verver in the second
volume of *The Golden Bowl*. The illicit passion which
disrupts her world is far closer to home, quite literally, than

that which Strether discovers: long before she finds the
golden bowl, the fact of the Prince's affair with Charlotte
has registered itself in the deepest parts of Maggie's psyche.
The Princess's awakening is thus not so much a question of
dramatic discovery as of the unfolding of knowledge from
within. And for the reader, the bipartite structure of the
novel intensifies this impression; in the second half of *The
Golden Bowl*, we watch Maggie uncover facts and feelings
which in the first half we have already—though but obscurely—known:

> They had got her into the bath and, for consistency with
> themselves—which was with each other—must keep her
> there. In that condition she wouldn't interfere with the
> policy, which was established, which was arranged. Her
> thought over this arrived at a great intensity—had indeed
> its pauses and timidities, but always to take afterwards
> a further and lighter spring. The ground was well-nigh
> covered by the time she had made out her husband and
> his colleague as directly interested in preventing her
> freedom of movement. Policy or no policy, it was they
> themselves who were arranged. She must be kept in
> position so as not to *dis*arrange them. It fitted immensely
> together, the whole thing, as soon as she could give them
> a motive; for, strangely as it had by this time begun
> to appear to herself, she hadn't hitherto imagined them
> sustained by an ideal distinguishably different from her
> own. Of course they were arranged—all four arranged;
> but what had the basis of their life been precisely but
> that they were arranged together? Ah! Amerigo and
> Charlotte were arranged together, but she—to confine
> the matter only to herself—was arranged apart. It rushed
> over her, the full sense of all this, with quite another
> rush from that of the breaking wave of ten days before;
> and as her father himself seemed not to meet the vaguely-
> clutching hand with which, during the first shock of
> complete perception, she tried to steady herself, so she
> felt very much alone.
>
> (24, IV, ii, pp. 44–45)

As Maggie begins to confront the design to which she has unconsciously surrendered her life, her thought has its "springs" as well as its "pauses and timidities." The language of Jamesian meditation dramatizes the compelling momentum with which the conscious mind, once awakened, enlarges its domain: by a strange mental fatality, to articulate one perception is to call forth in turn a host of others. Recognizing that the "policy" of Charlotte and the Prince is "established," Maggie's thought glides easily, as by the link of an appositive, to the perception that their policy is "arranged." But the safe neutrality of an "established" pattern slips quickly away: for the Princess to acknowledge that "arranging" is at issue here is to raise disturbing questions of power and control—to admit the fact of a particular "arrangement" and of particular motives in the arrangers. The beautiful Charlotte, her stepmother and best friend, now emerges in Maggie's mind as her husband's rather sinister "colleague"—joining with Amerigo in a design from which the Princess herself has been quite clearly excluded. "She must be kept in a position so as not to *dis*arrange them": with the simple addition of a mental prefix, the threat of discord breaks emphatically into Maggie's once charmed circle. In the time of her innocence, Maggie wistfully recalls, she had thought they were all four "arranged together," but even as she glances back at that easier past she is at once reminded of present pain. For to think in such terms is immediately to realize that only Charlotte and the Prince are in fact "together"; by an ironic corollary, Maggie must conclude that she herself has been "arranged" very much "apart." As each perception emerges into consciousness, it gives rise by a grim logic to the next: "the whole thing" fits "immensely"—and horribly—together.

To follow such a passage is to feel Maggie swept along by forces within herself which she cannot fully control. Insights are said to rush over her like "breaking waves," and knowledge comes as much by inner compulsion as by conscious choice. Maggie discovers the existence of a conspiracy here not by unearthing new facts, but by pursuing—or being pursued by—implications which subconsciously she has already half sensed. The association of words (as "arranged" suggests "*dis*arrange"; "together," "apart") and the forward thrust of syntax thus become for the reader analogues of the psyche's own drive toward consciousness. In the parenthetical interruption of a sentence we may sense that the Princess, like Strether, has her "pauses and timidities" ("but she—to confine the matter only to herself—"), but the sentence concludes nonetheless ("—was arranged apart"), the shock of complete perception making itself felt all the more strongly for the momentary delay. And even the gesture of mental postponement threatens, paradoxically, to become the means of revelation: by thinking in terms of confining matters to herself, Maggie implicitly acknowledges the very uneasiness about her father which she longs to suppress. For her desire not to know any more can only stem from her forebodings about what such further knowledge will be. Maggie's mental syntax is governed by the very paradoxes which will later endanger her precarious moment of communion with her father: ". . . it was as if they were 'in' for it, for something they had been ineffably avoiding, but the dread of which was itself in a manner a seduction, just as any confession of the dread was by so much an allusion" (24, V, iii, p. 265). Although James's *style indirect libre* keeps us at a certain distance from his men and women, we experience their shocks and fears with a peculiarly disturbing immediacy: the narrative style of the late novels acts as a powerful metaphor for the movement of the characters' troubled and painfully divided minds.

If the inhabitants of James's world so often dwell in a protracted state of innocence—extended in Strether's case for some "five-and-fifty" years—we nevertheless suspect that their resistance to experience is in direct proportion to their vast susceptibilities. For when he "lets himself go," it takes

rather little for the Jamesian character to find himself
carried away:

> The sense he had had before, the sense he had had re-
> peatedly, the sense that the situation was running away
> with him, had never been so sharp as now; and all the
> more that he could perfectly put his finger on the moment
> it had taken the bit in its teeth. That accident had
> definitely occurred, the other evening, after Chad's din-
> ner; it had occurred, as he fully knew, at the moment
> when he interposed between this lady and her child, when
> he suffered himself so to discuss with her a matter closely
> concerning them that her own subtlety, marked by its
> significant "Thank you!" instantly sealed the occasion in
> her favour. Again he had held off for ten days, but the
> situation had continued out of hand in spite of that;
> the fact that it was running so fast being indeed just *why*
> he had held off. What had come over him as he recog-
> nised her in the nave of the church was that holding off
> could be but a losing game from the instant she was
> worked for not only by her subtlety, but by the hand of
> fate itself. If all the accidents were to fight on her side —
> and by the actual showing they loomed large — he could
> only give himself up. This was what he had done in
> privately deciding then and there to propose she should
> breakfast with him. What did the success of his proposal
> in fact resemble but the smash in which a regular
> runaway properly ends? The smash was their walk, their
> déjeuner, their omelette, the Chablis, the place, the view,
> their present talk and his present pleasure in it — to
> say nothing, wonder of wonders, of her own. To this tune
> and nothing less, accordingly, was his surrender made
> good.
>
> (22, VII, i, pp. 14-15)

A tomato omelet, a bottle of wine, and "the mere way
Madame de Vionnet . . . thanked him for everything al-
most with the smile of a child" (p. 13), and the man from
Woollett comes to a smash; pleasantly dining with Chad's

mistress, Lambert Strether nonetheless feels himself a helpless victim of fate. But although the meeting with Marie de Vionnet in Notre Dame seems indeed an accident, surely no external force compelled Strether to succumb to her charms ten days earlier. He himself has issued the invitation to this delightful luncheon: the "situation" which now appears to run away with him is largely of his own making. James's characters, as his critics are so fond of pointing out, live in a world remarkably free from external compulsions (Kate Croy, relatively penniless, is perhaps an exception, but even Kate is at liberty to marry Densher and live in genteel poverty); if Strether is whirled along here by a metaphorical horse gone wild, that horse, like the pair in Plato's *Phaedrus*, is a purely psychic animal.

The image of the runaway is characteristically Jamesian, but even more characteristic is the way in which Strether grows conscious of his predicament: "the sense that the situation was running away with him" itself "runs away" with Strether's imagination — giving rise first to the image of an unnamed something with "the bit in its teeth," then to the recognition that he has "held off" precisely because it has been "running so fast," and finally to the vision of a conclusive smash. To feel as if something is "running away" with one is, after all, to feel in rather ordinary, even trite, terms: but in the Jamesian consciousness the implications of a buried metaphor have a striking habit of rising irresistibly to the surface and seeming to carry all before them. It is as if once Strether has consciously entertained the notion of running away, his imagination is indeed helpless — able to come to a halt only with "the smash in which a regular runaway properly ends." In the metaphoric sequence by which he is carried along we are made to feel how comically precarious is the balance of Strether's psyche. For although as usual he remains quite wide awake, the metamorphosis of his situation into a disastrous runaway proceeds by an oddly dreamlike logic. His thoughts do not run away with him strictly by free association of course: the buried meanings which surface in James's late novels seem to arise out of an

unconscious more cultural than personal—a shared unconscious of verbal origins and connections, not of private and
arbitrary associations. But the verbal drama here suggests
the psychic one; one process acts as a metaphor for the
other. For the Jamesian character is always in danger of
being tripped up by the laws of consciousness itself: in the
world of James's late fiction, buried meanings—like buried
facts and feelings—persistently disinter themselves.[10]

A fascination with concealed meanings lurking in well-
worn phrases, with dramatic plots which suddenly emerge
from cliché metaphors, runs in fact through all late Jamesian prose—nonfiction as well as fiction. And it has its
analogue as well in the Notebooks and Prefaces—in those
recurrent accounts of how buried "germs" of suggestion,
themselves often simple or trite, grew as if by their own
latent power into complex Jamesian fictions: "These are the
fascinations of the fabulist's art, these lurking forces of
expansion, these necessities of upspringing in the seed, these
beautiful determinations, on the part of the idea entertained, to grow as tall as possible, to push into the light and
the air and thickly flower there . . ." (Preface to *The
Portrait of a Lady, AN*, p. 42). Writing the history of his own
creations, James often makes himself seem not so much their
inventor as their discoverer—a man who chanced to stumble
upon already existing secrets and then had only to wait
while those secrets proceeded as if by magic to reveal
themselves:

> Never, positively, none the less, as the links multiplied,
> had I felt less stupid than for the determination of poor
> Strether's errand and for the apprehension of his issue.
> These things continued to fall together, as by the neat
> action of their own weight and form, even while their
> commentator scratched his head about them; he easily
> sees now that they were always well in advance of
> him. As the case completed itself he had in fact, from
> a good way behind, to catch up with them, breathless
> and a little flurried, as best he could.
>
> (*AN*, p. 315)

Its hidden pieces falling together, "as by the neat action of their own weight and form;" Strether's story seems to tell itself.

And so too do secrets persistently disclose themselves to characters in the late novels: Strether's encounter with Chad and Marie by the river or Maggie Verver's meeting with the antique dealer seems less the coincidence of plot than the inevitable surfacing of suppressed facts. Indeed one sometimes feels that Lord Mark in *The Wings of the Dove* exists less as a character in his own right than as the vehicle by which the lovers' clandestine plan may similarly reveal itself to Milly Theale, as it irresistibly emerges from the obscurity in which Kate and Densher have struggled so long to hide it. For if James is fascinated by the human need to suppress and conceal, his imagination is equally obsessed by the fateful process of disclosure—that mysterious law by which buried secrets phototropically seek "to push into the light and the air and thickly flower there."

Of course for James as author, the sense that his "germs" grew by themselves, that those carefully tended seeds had their own "necessities of upspringing," is in the end an illusion: *The Ambassadors* may have appeared to grow without its creator's active intervention, but the impulses that determined the pattern of Strether's adventures finally emerged from deep within James's self—from regions apparently inaccessible to conscious intention and control. The Preface offers a comic image—a vision of the poor "commentator" struggling to catch up with the consequences of his story—but the reality would make a more comic picture still: breathless, Our Author hastens to catch up with himself. For all its comedy, that imaginary picture of Henry James could well stand as a commentary on the strange and often tragic motions of his characters' minds.

When the secret of *The Wings of the Dove* finally discloses itself to Milly Theale, the American heiress "turns her face to the wall" and dies—thus suffering in an especially violent form the classic transition from innocence to experience. That painful transition is of course at the heart of Jamesian fiction: from *Roderick Hudson* and *The American* to *The Ambassadors* and *The Wings of the Dove*, James's innocent Americans travel to the continent of worldly experience, there to acquire a difficult and at times deadly knowledge. The journey from innocence to experience exercises a magnetic attraction on James's imagination; it is a story he tells again and again — even when he reverses the usual direction of the journey (*The Europeans, The Ivory Tower*), or allows his characters to venture only a short distance from home (as Mr. Longdon comes from the country to London in *The Awkward Age*, or the governess of *The Turn of the Screw* from her parsonage to Bly). Reduced to their barest outlines, James's tales repeatedly assume the shape of a secular Fall.

But if James's characters are doomed to lose their innocence, we still find it impossible to locate precisely the moment at which they eat of the tree of knowledge: the language of the late fiction suggests that the traditional account of that evil hour is indeed a myth. For in their encounters with experience the principal characters of the late novels undergo no sudden mutations. They are not like little Aggie in *The Awkward Age* — an apparent innocent who plummets abruptly, once licensed by marriage, into a state of depraved knowledge. Much more closely do they resemble Nanda Brookenham, who for as long as we know her "struggle[s] with instincts and forebodings, with the suspicion of . . . doom and the far-borne scent, in the flowery fields, of blood" (9, V, iii, p. 239). The late style makes of the Fall into knowledge not a dramatic reversal, but a gradual unfolding — an unfolding from the depths of the psyche itself. Knowledge does not come as a sudden violation of the self from an exterior and alien world: the late novels have their climactic moments of discovery, but in those moments James's men and women confront what in some part of themselves they have long since known. Like

Milton's Adam and Eve, even the most innocent of James's characters are never quite unfallen.

In *The Turn of the Screw*, that endlessly problematic ghost story which so closely precedes the major phase, the ambiguities of fallen knowledge haunt governess and reader alike: Are the children innocent and in what sense? How much do they really "know"? If by the end of the tale they are indeed fallen creatures, when did their fall take place — when Peter Quint and Miss Jessel were alive or more recently, under the terrifying pressures and demands of the governess herself?[11] At the emotional center of all this ghostly intrigue is the adult's dread of that terrible knowingness children seem to possess — a source of anxiety to which James likewise turned in each of the novels which surround his "fairy-tale" (Preface to *The Aspern Papers, AN*, p. 171). For in both *What Maisie Knew* and *The Awkward Age* he chose as his subject a young girl, hovering uneasily between the innocence of childhood and a mature knowledge of the world's evil. Maisie Farange is somewhat younger than Nanda Brookenham, but that precocious child must suffer as much as Nanda herself through the torments of an "awkward age": "It was to be the fate of this patient little girl," James writes of Maisie, "to see much more than she at first understood, but also even at first to understand much more than any little girl, however patient, had perhaps ever understood before" (11, i, p. 9). As that time in which the mind is uncomfortably suspended somewhere in the obscurity between childish apprehensions and adult knowledge, adolescence has for James a predictable fascination. If "the infant mind would at the best leave great gaps and voids," as he says in the Preface to *Maisie* (*AN*, p. 145), the grown minds of the late novels have "gaps and voids" as well — vacancies of conscious awareness which they often strive very hard not to fill. Sensing much more than he is yet psychically able to acknowledge, Strether at fifty-five suffers a crisis remarkably like that of adolescence: in the children of the 1890s James directly anticipates the bewilderment of his twentieth-century adults.

And to read the late novels is at least temporarily to share some of that bewilderment. For like the characters, we too are continuously forced to hover somewhere between ignorance and full knowledge, to struggle with intimations and possibilities which make themselves but obliquely felt. The late style demands that at every point we sense more than we are yet able to articulate; only gradually do we grow fully conscious of our own subliminal guesses. In *The Wings of the Dove*, it is not until Milly's Venetian party — more than three-quarters of the way through the novel (20, VIII, iii) — that Kate and Densher finally make their intentions toward Milly explicit. Yet like Strether by the river or Densher himself at this moment, the sensitive reader must respond to their words with a feeling closer to recognition than to shock. Though we would find it impossible to locate the precise moment in the past at which we learned the truth about the lovers' plans, we are nevertheless likely to feel as if we have long known just what the lovers had in mind. It seems as if the truth has been latent in the situation from the very beginning and that we have always subconsciously sensed it: like the characters, we feel that in discovering the truth we thus discover some part of ourselves.

In an early review of George Eliot's novels, James lamented the author's decision to conclude *Adam Bede* by directly informing her readers of Adam's marriage to Dinah Morris: "The assurance of this possibility," James wrote, "is what I should have desired the author to place the sympathetic reader at a standpoint to deduce for himself." For the novelist must compel his reader to join in the labor of the novel: "In every novel the work is divided between the writer and the reader; but the writer makes the reader very much as he makes his characters. When he makes him ill, that is, makes him indifferent, he does no work; the writer does all. When he makes him well, that is, makes him interested, then the reader does quite half the labour."[12] In the world of his own late fiction, facts rarely seem as solid and unequivocal as the union of Eliot's sturdy carpenter and his Methodist bride; nor are they usually so consoling. The style of James's late novels makes the reader work not only to deduce unstated possibilities but to fathom minds which are themselves both attracted and repelled by these very possibilities — minds in which conscious recognitions and unconscious pressures are continually at war. In his late fiction James does indeed "make the reader very much as he makes his characters": the fascination of knowledge — and some measure of the fear — becomes the reader's own. And in guessing at the facts, in trying to make conscious and explicit all that the characters themselves fear to think and speak, we may conclude by writing our own fictions — ending our search for the truth, strangely enough, where James's characters so often begin: in the realm of metaphor.

3   The Imagination of Metaphor

In *The Beast in the Jungle*, that late *nouvelle* whose theme tragically mirrors that of *The Ambassadors*, James creates a man obsessed with a metaphor. John Marcher, the tale's antihero, is convinced that "something or other . . . [lies] in wait for him, amid the twists and turns of the months and years, like a crouching beast in the jungle" (17, ii, p. 79). Living in anxious expectation, he awaits the "inevitable spring" of the metaphoric beast—the moment at which his long-awaited destiny will manifest itself, and "*the* thing" (i, p. 73) at last come upon him. Beneath the outwardly dull surface of his existence, Marcher stalks his beast like a man on a "tiger hunt." At least, "such was the image under which he had ended by figuring his life" (ii, p. 79).

But Marcher the tiger-hunter is in reality Marcher the terrified. The image which haunts him implies a readiness to confront exotic horrors, but all the while that he pursues his beast, Marcher flees in terror from ordinary human contact and from love. On a late April afternoon in a quiet London town house, May Bartram offers herself to him; but Marcher, obsessed with metaphors of distant jungles and mysterious beasts, utterly fails to understand what is happening. Through the metaphor of the beast in the jungle, apparently a talisman of hidden knowledge, Marcher actually retreats from knowledge—both sexual knowledge of May and conscious knowledge of himself. Metaphoric thinking allows him to evade immediate reality and its demands, to avoid the risk of passionate confrontation.

Yet even the frustratingly obtuse Marcher at last comes to

perceive the pattern of his life, to understand the meaning of his escape and his loss. After May Bartram has died, Marcher haunts her grave, and it is during one such autumn vigil that the truth finally dawns. Shocked into awareness by the grief-stricken face of a fellow visitor to the graveyard, by "the deep ravage of the features he showed" (vi, p. 123), Marcher asks himself, "What had the man *had,* to make him by the loss of it so bleed and yet live?" (p. 124). In typically Jamesian fashion, the very form of the question calls forth the answer: "Something—and this reached him with a pang—that *he,* John Marcher, hadn't; the proof of which was precisely John Marcher's arid end. No passion had ever touched him, for this was what passion meant; he had survived and maundered and pined, but where had been *his* deep ravage?" Too late comes "the truth, vivid and monstrous" (p. 125); in this long-delayed moment of illumination Marcher finally grasps the missing tenor of his metaphor:

> The Beast had lurked indeed, and the Beast, at its hour, had sprung; it had sprung in that twilight of the cold April when, pale, ill, wasted, but all beautiful, and perhaps even then recoverable, she had risen from her chair to stand before him and let him imaginably guess. It had sprung as he didn't guess; it had sprung as she hopelessly turned from him, and the mark, by the time he left her, had fallen where it *was* to fall. He had justified his fear and achieved his fate; he had failed, with the last exactitude, of all he was to fail of; and a moan now rose to his lips as he remembered she had prayed he mightn't know. This horror of waking—*this* was knowledge, knowledge under the breath of which the very tears in his eyes seemed to freeze.
>
> (vi, p. 126)

The exotic is brought home, and in this painful moment of awakening Marcher recognizes that May's offer of love and his own failure to respond marked the true spring of the beast. Paradoxically, the metaphor through which Marcher has escaped comes in the end to signify both the experience which he fled and the very flight itself. The beast sprang when May made her humble gesture of love; it sprang again when the self-absorbed Marcher failed to comprehend her gesture. And it springs once more, most horrifyingly, at this final moment of full awareness: "He saw the Jungle of his life and saw the lurking Beast; then, while he looked, perceived it, as by a stir of the air, rise, huge and hideous, for the leap that was to settle him. His eyes darkened—it was close; and instinctively turning, in his hallucination, to avoid it, he flung himself, face down, on the tomb" (vi, pp. 126—27). Marcher's beast—a distant cousin of that tiger with the gleaming eyes which in *Death in Venice* crouches in Aschenbach's hallucinatory jungle[1]—is at once sensual love, the failure of self-knowledge, and the pain of that knowledge come too late.

Marcher clings to his metaphor in order to distance reality, to postpone the anguish of knowledge, but when knowledge at last overwhelms him, the metaphor turns sickeningly real; the beast which leaps in the final lines of James's tale may be hallucinatory, but for Marcher the effect of its last spring is a condition virtually indistinguishable from death. So too does discovery come in *The Wings of the Dove*, where Milly Theale's enlightenment proves even more unmistakably fatal: while the disease from which the American heiress suffers remains mysterious, the revelation about Kate and Densher nonetheless kills. In the late novels knowledge comes, even to the apparently healthy, with a terrible fatality. And metaphors, as ways of mediating that dangerous knowledge, assume a new and crucial power. Unlike James's early novels, whose titles point to literal people (*Roderick Hudson*), places (*Washington Square*), or cultures (*The American, The Europeans, The Bostonians*), the late novels are identified not by character or location, but by image and symbol (*The Sacred Fount, The Wings of the Dove, The Golden Bowl, The Ivory Tower*).[2] Experience itself now has—indeed for James's characters, it must have—a metaphoric name.[3]

Of course the unsuspecting reader who came across *The*

Beast in the Jungle and, easily misled by metaphor, expected to find a dramatic tale of tiger-hunting in the African jungle—or at least a narrative with the outward adventure of Marlowe's in *Heart of Darkness*—would suffer sharp disappointment. For *The Beast in the Jungle* is the story of a man who, as he himself comes too late to realize, has been "*the* man, to whom nothing on earth was to have happened" (vi, 125). As such, it is almost a parody of the classic Jamesian plot, and Marcher, that sensitive, passive, and deeply reserved gentleman, is the quintessential Jamesian hero—both plot and character unfortunately apt to make the impatient reader of James cringe. But even essentially responsive readers are likely to find the gross disproportion between Marcher and his metaphor obscurely disquieting, to sense beneath the surface a tension and a strain not easily accounted for. Like so many late Jamesian metaphors, Marcher's obsessive imagery arouses in us a persistent unease.

Indeed at their most characteristic, James's metaphors provoke a feeling of arbitrariness and extravagance, a sense of an uncomfortable break in the organic connection of things, that can be deeply disturbing. To F. R. Leavis, for example, this strain in the late imagery betrays the decline of James's art, signals the Master's final loss of poetic power: "We are conscious in these figures more of analysis, demonstration and comment than of the realizing imagination and the play of poetic perception. Between any original perception or feeling there may have been and what we're given there has come a process of judicial stock-taking; the imagery is not immediate and inevitable but synthetic. It is diagrammatic rather than poetic."[4] And even one of James's most sympathetic critics finds herself forced to condemn the more extreme images in *The Golden Bowl* as "arbitrary" and "heavy-handed."[5] Others, simply ignoring the problem, content themselves with explicating individual metaphors as they arise, or with classifying them by vehicle—informing us, for example, that one can count more than thirteen hundred water images in James's fiction.[6] But no matter how much water imagery we can find flooding James's pages, our sense of disquietude remains: the tension generated by many of James's later metaphors does not so easily wash away. And if the strange connections between jungle beasts and civil servants continue to puzzle and disturb, they continue to haunt us as well — to exert on us their own fearful fascinations.

Some of our unease — Leavis's sense that the imagery is not "immediate and inevitable" — stems from the fact that James's metaphors seem almost invariably responses of the brain, not of the senses. The Jamesian universe is not one of material resemblances; though the vehicles of his metaphors are themselves sensuously imagined, conceptual relationships govern the terms of comparison. The Venetian weather in *The Wings of the Dove* is "a bath of warm air" (20, IX, iv, p. 304), Paris has "a cool full studio-light" in *The Ambassadors* (22, VIII, ii, p. 76), and little Bilham shakes his ears "in the manner of a terrier who has got wet" (22, X, i, p. 173), but such physical comparisons are only occasional and incidental. Perception of sensuous correspondences is direct and immediate, but the world of the late novels does not allow of such easy connections among its parts. Even for Strether, whose education in Paris is so much an affair of the senses, perception is primarily cognition, and — perhaps especially for Strether — the correspondences between things take considerable working out.

In *The Golden Bowl*, Maggie Verver, like little Bilham, is compared to a wet dog shaking itself out; but unlike little Bilham's, her resemblance to the dog is not a physical one:

> Moving for the first time in her life as in the darkening shadow of a false position, she reflected that she should either not have ceased to be right — that is to be confident — or have recognised that she was wrong; though she tried to deal with herself for a space only as a silken-coated spaniel who has scrambled out of a pond

and who rattles the water from his ears. Her shake of her head, again and again, as she went, was much of that order, and she had the resource to which, save for the rude equivalent of his generalising bark, the spaniel would have been a stranger, of humming to herself hard as a sign that nothing had happened to her. She hadn't, so to speak, fallen in; she had had no accident nor got wet; this at any rate was her pretension until after she began a little to wonder if she mightn't, with or without exposure, have taken cold.

(24, IV, i, pp. 6–7)

This metaphoric spaniel makes its appearance near the opening of the novel's second volume, as Maggie Verver, slowly awakening from her dream of innocence, begins to sense that all is not well with her world. No inherent resemblance links a wet spaniel and a young woman awakening to a knowledge of evil; the connection is not apparent until it is made, until dog and girl are brought in conjunction and their resemblances defined. Maggie is said to give a "shake of her head"—a shake itself ambiguously metaphoric or literal, but it is not physical gesture or appearance which makes her spaniel-like: there is no question here of puppy-dog eyes or barking voices, although the young Princess perhaps shares with the spaniel a "silken coat." It is Maggie's whole state of consciousness which is likened to the shaking dog.

At this point in her history, Maggie knows nothing—consciously at least—about her husband's adultery with Charlotte, or about her own responsibility for the evil which has entered her world. She knows only that she has begun to feel distinctly uneasy; she is as yet far from knowing why. And she is frightened—frightened both of the feeling itself and of inquiring too closely into its causes. Suspecting unpleasant truths, like falling into the water, is a discomforting experience, and in metaphorically shaking herself dry, Maggie tries to reject that experience, to deny that she is in any way afraid. The desire to suppress her agitating suspicions runs deep:

"She hadn't , so to speak, fallen in; she had had no accident nor got wet." But even more crucial than this metaphoric gesture is the fact of the metaphor itself — Maggie thinks not of painful human relationships but of a spaniel which has tumbled into a pond. The image of the wet dog allows her to avoid direct confrontation with the truth and to post-pone the anguish which that truth may bring. Though it is a far less sinister creature, Maggie's spaniel is of the same species as Marcher's jungle beast.

Unlike Marcher, however, Maggie begins to face reality, not to flee from it. And her metaphoric thinking, though it is a means of evasion, is also a mode of discovery. Although she postpones full knowledge, wishing simply to shake off her uneasiness as if it were water, the process of image-making has a momentum of its own. One association suggests another; to juxtapose in the mind a wet spaniel and an apprehensive young princess is apparently to see more resemblances between them than one had originally bar-gained for. Thus even as Maggie denies her likeness to the dog, she does so in the metaphor's own terms: "She hadn't, so to speak, fallen in; she had had no accident nor got wet." And "so to speak" is to carry out the metaphor to its natural conclusion: like the spaniel, Maggie realizes, she too may have "taken cold." Falling into water can precipitate a cold — it is as though the common-sense associations of the metaphor had forced Maggie to acknowledge that she cannot completely suppress the psychic chills she has begun to feel.

But if Maggie begins "a little to wonder" whether she has "taken cold," she is not yet ready to translate the implica-tions of her metaphor into a direct comment on her situation. She thinks in terms of taking cold, not in terms of psychic threats; the language which defines her new aware-ness remains in the context of metaphor rather than of fact. And the metaphor itself suggests meanings which Maggie at this point cannot consciously articulate. It is not fortuitous that she sees herself as a spaniel and not some other wet animal, for example; unconsciously, at least, she presumably senses a resemblance between the pliable, fawning nature of a spaniel and her own susceptibility to use and deception. Maggie knows more than she knows she knows, and her metaphor mediates between conscious knowledge and deeper modes of awareness.

For the Princess to approach the tangle of her husband's unfaithfulness, Charlotte's treachery, and her own reprehensible innocence by means of a wet spaniel is to take a devious route indeed. That her metaphoric vehicle nevertheless carries her in the direction of the truth comes to both Maggie and the reader with something of a metaphysical shock; [7] like Dr. Johnson confronted with the imagery of the seventeenth-century poets, we may well wonder at the "violence" with which these heterogeneous ideas are yoked together. Maggie's situation bears no more immediate resemblance to that of a wet dog than do Donne's two lovers to a pair of compasses. [8]

Of course in "A Valediction: Forbidding Mourning," that paradigm of all metaphysical poems, the speaker's self-conscious wit is the violently yoking force; he takes an active delight in his imaginative exercise, wittily uncovering multiple resemblances where none would at first seem to exist. And as the language of a departing lover, trying to assure both himself and his beloved of the permanence of their union, this play with metaphor serves an urgent rhetorical function. The compasses image does not merely illustrate the lover's argument: rather, it *is* his argument — an imagistic proof that physical separation will not destroy his connection with the beloved. The more analogies he can draw between compasses and lovers, the more convincing his case. The elaboration of his metaphor becomes an assertion of control over a potentially threatening experience, a means of shaping language and love affair alike.

When Maggie makes the metaphysical leap between herself and the spaniel, she is not, like Donne's persona, engaged in a direct rhetorical argument. She has no need to prove anything or to persuade anyone—anyone, that is, except herself. Maggie's meditation is not even spoken aloud, but beneath its surface an argument nevertheless takes place, although the parties to the conflict do not exist as separate persons at all and are not in fact easily distinguishable from one another. Self argues with self within Maggie Verver, as her deep fear of the truth contends with her strong need to know where she stands, as her uneasy suspicions arise, are suppressed, and irresistibly surface once again. And in this struggle, each side claims the metaphor for its own and uses it rhetorically, if the parts of the self can be said to engage in a kind of subconscious rhetoric. "I have not, so to speak, fallen in; I have had no accident nor got wet," insists the fearful self, extending the metaphor negatively, and thus "proving" that Maggie has no reason to be afraid. "Ah, but do you not feel as if you had in fact taken cold?" returns the other self, triumphantly reasserting the sinister possibilities inherent in the original image and forcing Maggie to acknowledge, at least metaphorically, the pain which she has begun to feel.

No such dialogue takes place, of course. Nor does Maggie's psyche so neatly divide into two equal and opposing parts. We read the passage as one continuous meditation and recognize only one consciousness at work (to ignore, for the moment, the hovering consciousness of the narrator himself). But the conflict which such a dialogue would overtly dramatize is genuine and accounts for much of the tension which we experience as we read. Though Maggie at this point knows so little of the actual facts of the case, her struggle is already intense—finally all the more intense for us as readers because we are not allowed the relief of direct statement. Like so much in late James, her conflict makes itself felt only obliquely, exerting its pressure through the indirection of style.

The sense of shock with which Dr. Johnson would have greeted Maggie and her incongruous spaniel is a feeling which all readers of the late James can appreciate, even if,

F. R. Leavis apart, most of us are no longer prepared to condemn such incongruity as a stylistic flaw. The disparity between vehicle and tenor which makes so many of James's late images metaphysically surprising suggests a world in which connections are not easily made, one in which the imagination must strain to see the resemblances of things. In some instances (such as the comparison of Maggie to the spaniel or the Prince's extended contrast between himself as a *crême de volaille* and Adam Verver as "the natural fowl running about the *bassecour*" [23, I, i, p. 8]) the vehicles of such metaphors startle by their very homeliness; at other points they shock by the melodramatic and even violent situations which they conjure up (Maggie as a victim of the French Revolution, awaiting execution [24, VI, ii, pp. 341–42]; or Milly Theale's clinging to the Rockies for dear life [19, V, vii, p. 302]), or simply by their air of exotic mystery (Maggie's pagoda or Milly Theale's eastern carpet [19, V, i, p. 216]). The strangeness of these vehicles resembles the strangeness of dreams—at once distant and bizarre, seemingly far removed from ordinary life, and startlingly immediate in their implications. Denied the ordinary dreams of sleep, James's characters appear to find in their waking imagery an equivalent release.

Yet the uneasiness which James's late images may evoke does not arise simply from the shock of heterogeneity but from the elaboration and extension of the original metaphor—what Dr. Leavis, that latter-day Dr. Johnson, calls "analysis, demonstration and comment" as opposed to "the realizing imagination and the play of poetic perception." The famous image of the pagoda which opens the second volume of *The Golden Bowl* is a troublesome case in point. Even Dorothea Krook, usually so responsive to the late James, has objected to this oriental oddity, and to the lengthy mental journeys by which Maggie approaches it: " . . . the oddness of the image is felt to be in excess of the originality of the experience, making it in this sense arbitrary; and its disproportionate and rather heavy-handed protraction noticeably slackens the dramatic pace at the point at which it occurs."[9] But the very oddness of this protracted image is crucial, forcing to our attention emotional strains which a more comfortable metaphor would fail to convey. To discover that one's husband is an adulterer may not, unfortunately, be a particularly original experience, although Maggie is far from realizing that adultery is even in question. But the originality of the image makes of the experience something rich and strange, tells us that for Maggie what is at stake here is indeed profoundly unusual and disturbing:

> This situation had been occupying for months and months the very centre of the garden of her life, but it had reared itself there like some strange tall tower of ivory, or perhaps rather some wonderful beautiful but outlandish pagoda, a structure plated with hard bright porcelain, coloured and figured and adorned at the overhanging eaves with silver bells that tinkled ever so charmingly when stirred by chance airs. She had walked round and round it — that was what she felt; she had carried on her existence in the space left her for circulation, a space that sometimes seemed ample and sometimes narrow: looking up all the while at the fair structure that spread itself so amply and rose so high, but never quite making out as yet where she might have entered had she wished. She hadn't wished till now — such was the odd case. . . . The thing might have been, by the distance at which it kept her, a Mahometan mosque, with which no base heretic could take a liberty; there so hung about it the vision of one's putting off one's shoes to enter and even verily of one's paying with one's life if found there as an interloper. She hadn't certainly arrived at the conception of paying with her life for anything she might do; but it was nevertheless quite as if she had sounded with a tap or two one of the rare porcelain plates.
>
> (24, IV, i, pp. 3–4)

The "outlandish" pagoda which sits in Maggie's Eden-like garden is an emblem of the bizarre social "arrangement" which has heretofore governed her life, but for us it might figure as well the entire world of James's late novels—a world of bright and intricate surfaces, extraordinarily beautiful and yet ominously "hard," concealing mysterious and possibly sinister depths. To Maggie the tower seems to have "reared itself," with a power that architectural monuments possess solely in dreams; knowing herself simply as passive and innocent, she cannot yet perceive her own complicity in the architecture of her past, nor assume active responsibility for the future design of her life. The peculiar arbitrariness and artifice of the pagoda image reflect her estrangement from the reality of her situation, the fact that for the innocent Princess the truths of her own life have all the mystery of the inscrutable Orient.[10]

Yet for the first time Maggie has become aware of a desire, however hesitant, to penetrate that mystery. At once fascinated and terrified, she anxiously circles around the pagoda, venturing at last to administer a tentative "tap or two" on its hard and unyielding surface. "She had knocked, in short—though she could scarce have said whether for admission or for what . . ." (p. 4). Even as she circles around the tower, so she circles around the metaphor itself— tentatively exploring each of its implications in turn, only to shrink back in fear when that exploration leads her in directions more dangerous than she is yet prepared to move. The pagoda may suggest a Mahometan mosque, threatening death to all interlopers, but "she hadn't certainly arrived at the conception of paying with her life for anything she might do." To argue that the prolongation of the metaphor "slackens the dramatic pace" is thus to measure the speed of Maggie's mind by a completely alien clock, for the dramatic pace at this point is precisely one of hesitant and fearful groping for knowledge rather than of sudden and blinding revelation. Eve may have acquired knowledge with a single bite of the apple, but for Maggie Verver—as for so many of James's late characters—the fall from innocence has become a painfully drawn-out process. Though Maggie will seem to awaken, in Fanny Assingham's words, "to what's called Evil—with a very big E" (23, III, xi, p. 385), she will really discover a world to which the clear-cut terms of good and evil no longer apply—a world of ambiguities and fearful mysteries, one in which knowledge itself must remain finally tentative and uncertain. And only through metaphoric indirection can such knowledge even be approached.

If the metaphysical extension of this exotic metaphor recalls the lyric poetry of the seventeenth century rather than the novelistic tradition of the nineteenth, the resemblance is not purely fortuitous. For the world of James's late fiction is an intensely private one—a world in which the individual consciousness must struggle, alone, to articulate the connections of things. To restrict point of view as radically as James does is to create characters who must perforce suffer a certain isolation, and the private elaboration of metaphor confirms that isolation. Like her nineteenth-century predecessor, George Eliot's Dorothea Brooke, Maggie Verver must awaken from a state of innocence to discover a deeply flawed marriage, and to acknowledge her own responsibility for its failure. But the metaphysical imagery which surrounds Maggie's awakening suggests that James's heroine must confront more than a failed marriage: she must puzzle out the very terms of her world anew.

In *Middlemarch,* when Dorothea Brooke begins to sense the truth about the aging, desiccated scholar whom she has married, she sees herself as entrapped in the narrow and oppressive labyrinths of his mind: "How was it that in the weeks since her marriage, Dorothea had not distinctly observed but felt with a stifling depression, that the large vistas and wide fresh air which she had dreamed of finding in her husband's mind were replaced by anterooms and winding passages which seemed to lead nowither?" Nothing more comes of these anterooms and winding passages at this particular point; the metaphor, like the passages themselves, leads nowhere. Instead, the omnipresent voice of the narrator immediately intrudes with analogous metaphors of her own:

> I suppose it was that in courtship everything is regarded as provisional and preliminary, and the smallest sample of virtue or accomplishment is taken to guarantee delightful stores which the broad leisure of marriage will reveal. But the door-sill of marriage once crossed, expectation is concentrated on the present. Having once embarked on your marital voyage, it is impossible not to be aware that you make no way and that the sea is not within sight — that, in fact, you are exploring an enclosed basin.[11]

Blocked passageways, door-sills, enclosed basins — Eliot's metaphors in *Middlemarch* proceed by analogy, and Dorothea's image gains in resonance from the larger pattern of labyrinths and enclosures of which it forms a part.[12] Even so does Dorothea herself fit into the larger design of Middlemarch society — here reminding us strongly of Lydgate or even of Fred Vincy, there contrasting sharply with Rosamond or with Mary Garth. In *Middlemarch* the individual metaphor, like the individual character, derives much of its significance from its relation to others of its kind. Unlike Maggie Verver, Dorothea Brooke does not stand alone in the world of her novel: Lydgate, Fred, Rosamond, Bulstrode, and a host of minor characters all mirror her experience of frustrated expectation, and even the narrator clearly echoes and confirms her metaphors.

One imagines that if *Middlemarch* were a late James novel, Dorothea would have entered the anterooms of Casaubon's mind and explored its dark and winding passages — only to find herself, apparently trapped, searching desperately for an exit, some glimmer of light to suggest that not all her husband's mental passageways had dead ends. Even as early as *The Portrait of a Lady*, in fact, James sends his heroine on just such an extended metaphorical journey.[13] Like Dorothea Brooke, Isabel Archer confronts the disappointing truth of her marriage, and like Dorothea, she finds not the vast expanses she had imagined, but only narrow alleys and dead walls:

> She had taken all the first steps in the purest confidence, and then she had suddenly found the infinite vista of a multiplied life to be a dark, narrow alley with a dead wall at the end. Instead of leading to the high places of happiness, from which the world would seem to lie below one, so that one could look down with a sense of exaltation and advantage, and judge and choose and pity, it led rather downward and earthward, into realms of restriction and depression, where the sound of other lives, easier and freer, was heard as from above, and served to deepen the feeling of failure.
>
> (xlii, pp. 371-72)

Both Isabel and Dorothea come to metaphoric dead ends, but in James's novel the metaphor itself continues to expand. In *Middlemarch* metaphors, like people, exist in analogical relationship to one another, bound by a common pattern, but in the second half of her novel Isabel Archer stands very much alone. Her metaphor extends itself vertically, not horizontally: in private meditation its meanings unfold.

The world of James's cosmopolites and expatriates is far from the provincial town of Middlemarch, with its closely knit web of relationships and metaphoric resemblances. But James's characters, though deeply lonely, live in a world inhabited by others, and when they come into contact with one another, they talk. Strether's falling in love with Paris or Kate's and Densher's with each other, for example, is partly a question of good conversation, of the satisfying exchange of thoughts ("It had come to be definite between them [Kate and Densher] at a primary stage that, if they could have no other straight way, the realm of thought at least was open to them. They could think whatever they liked about whatever they would — in other words they could say it. Saying it for each other, for each other alone, only of course added to the taste" [19, II, i, p. 65]). And much Jamesian conversation is the mutual creation of metaphor:

> "Mrs. Pocock's built in, or built out — whichever you call it; she's packed so tight she can't move. She's in splendid isolation" — Miss Barrace embroidered the theme.
>
> Strether followed, but scrupulous of justice. "Yet with every one in the place successively introduced to her."
>
> "Wonderfully — but just so that it does build her out. She's bricked up, she's buried alive!"
>
> Strether seemed for a moment to look at it; but it brought him to a sigh. "Oh but she's not dead! It will take more than this to kill her."
>
> His companion had a pause that might have been for pity. "No, I can't pretend I think she's finished — or that it's for more than to-night." She remained pensive as if with the same compunction. "It's only up to her chin." Then again for the fun of it: "She can breathe."
>
> "She can breathe!" — he echoed it in the same spirit. "And do you know," he went on, "what's really all this time happening to me? — through the beauty of music, the gaiety of voices, the uproar in short of our revel and the felicity of your wit? The sound of Mrs. Pocock's respiration drowns for me, I assure you, every other. It's literally all I hear."
>
> She focussed him with her clink of chains. "Well—!" she breathed ever so kindly.
>
> "Well, what?"
>
> "She *is* free from her chin up," she mused; "and that *will* be enough for her."
>
> "It will be enough for me!" Strether ruefully laughed.
>
> (*The Ambassadors*, 22, X, i, pp. 176–77)

Strether and Miss Barrace join in this verbal game-playing partly "for the fun of it"; Miss Barrace, in fact, with her cigarette-smoking and her ironic banter, incarnates that spirit of frivolous wit which both charms and frightens Strether in his Parisian friends. And certainly there is much here both to charm and to frighten, for if the tone of the exchange is lighthearted, ominous implications lurk beneath its surface. Sarah Pocock, outwardly presiding at a fes-

tive party given in her honor, is in metaphorical fact being
"buried alive." And despite the "uproar" of music and party
chatter, Strether can hear only the imagined sound of her
breathing—so alarming a force does Mrs. Pocock represent
for him that the mere fact of her presence obliterates all
else.

In this joint image-making, Strether and Miss Barrace act
both as friendly collaborators and as conspirators. For
speaking in metaphors, like thinking in metaphors, is a way
at once of confronting and of avoiding unpleasant facts; by
inventing this grotesque image of Sarah "packed so tight she
can't move," they manage to acknowledge Strether's hidden
anxiety and yet to hold it at a safely comic distance. The
incongruity of the metaphor itself is matched by the incongruity between the gay social surface of this conversation
and the tensions it only partly conceals. And the very
elaboration of the image intensifies the disparity, for in
playfully extending their metaphor, Strether and his companion assert a kind of witty verbal control over the entire
uneasy situation, even while they call heightened attention
to it: by the end of the exchange the ominous breathing of
Mrs. Pocock is very much in the air. At a Jamesian party, to
play with metaphors is to risk being surprised into uncomfortable truths.

But Strether's uncomfortable truths, troubling as they
often are, are only metaphorically questions of life and
death. Given what we know of the redoubtable Mrs. Pocock,
we need have little fear that she will literally be buried alive.
Unlike *The Wings of the Dove*, *The Ambassadors* has no
Milly Theale, who dies a quite literal, though intensely
symbolic death. And unlike Maggie Verver in *The Golden
Bowl*, Strether is not the immediate victim of the adultery
which he uncovers. Like his feminine counterparts, he is
betrayed by a pair of lovers, but unlike Milly and Maggie,
Strether remains something of a detached observer of
events, rather than an anguished participant in them.
Although his journey to Paris deprives him of his innocence
and radically transforms his way of seeing things, the facts

which Strether must confront are not as directly threatening
or as powerfully disturbing as those with which Milly Theale
or Maggie Verver must finally come to terms. *The Ambassadors*, with its detached and frequently ironic tone, is, in
fact, the most comic of the three late novels—and the least
metaphoric.[14] For in James's late fiction, the metaphoric
imagination works with its most feverish intensity when
faced with knowledge that is both deeply desired and
profoundly terrifying.

In *The Wings of the Dove*, the love affair between Merton
Densher and Kate Croy calls forth precisely such desires and
such terrors, as even their seemingly innocent metaphors
may reveal: "You keep the key of the cupboard, and I
foresee that when we're married you'll dole me out my sugar
by lumps," says Densher to Kate in an early, relatively
untroubled moment. Indeed, we are told that this sweetly
domestic image has sprung to Densher's lips "more than
once" in their brief acquaintance (20, VI, ii, p. 17)—an
assertion which may strain our credulity in realistic terms
but which suggests that the metaphoric key to the cupboard
is a key to the nature of their relationship as well. Characteristically, Kate chooses to make explicit only the sweetness of
the image: "she rejoiced in his assumption that sugar would
be his diet." But for Densher, the reader suspects, the sweet
overtones of the metaphor mask a taste of bitterness. Listening to Kate's confident pronouncements on the problem of their finding a satisfactory place to meet one another,
he has tentatively admitted to himself a certain misgiving:
"what Kate embraced altogether was indeed wonderful . . .
though he perhaps struck himself rather as getting it out of
her piece by piece than as receiving it in a steady light" (20,
VI, ii, p. 16). Despite all the sweetness and light with which
he associates her, and despite the hesitant "perhaps" and
"rather," a spot of ambivalence creeps into Densher's picture
of the "bright and handsome" Kate.

But like Maggie Verver at the opening of the second
volume of *The Golden Bowl*, Densher at this point can only

approach his own anxieties with timid indirection — extending the metaphor of the locked cupboard and the sugar lumps no further than a cautious negative will allow: "the supply from the cupboard at this hour was doubtless, of a truth, not altogether cloyingly sweet; but it met in a manner his immediate requirements" (20, VI, ii, p. 17). The image's more sinister implications — of Kate's arbitrary power and Densher's willful ignorance — go unexplored. It remains for the reader himself to pursue the logic of the metaphor and to wonder what else lies behind the locked doors of Kate's cupboard.

That closed cupboard might stand in fact as an emblem of the entire history of this passionate conspiracy. Until the final scenes of the novel, when Milly's death forces him to confront the full significance of what they have done, Densher will prefer to keep many of his mental cupboards locked, passively allowing Kate to assume charge of the keys. And she will respond by doling him out his lumps of sugar — offering him, bit by bit, only palatable interpretations of their acts, interpretations which he can pleasantly swallow, and holding back anything which might strike his moral palate as bitter. If Strether and Maggie Verver often act as their own censors, Densher frequently surrenders the role to Kate, allowing her to suppress the darker implications of a metaphor, and thus to save him from the terror of conscious self-knowledge.

Shaping metaphors, then, becomes a means of control; Kate avoids any overt disharmony in her relationship with Densher by acknowledging only the sweeter implications of his images. But in *The Wings of the Dove*, at least, a strange shift of power takes place: by the end of the novel, the living woman, Kate Croy, must step aside for the dead Milly Theale. And Milly triumphs not so much by inventing metaphors of her own as by adopting and transforming the metaphors of others. When Kate, with characteristic ambiguity, pronounces her a "dove," Milly welcomes the image as if it were a divine revelation, immediately adopting it as her own:

It was moreover, for the girl, like an inspiration: she found herself accepting as the right one, while she caught her breath with relief, the name so given her. She met it on the instant as she would have met revealed truth; it lighted up the strange dusk in which she lately had walked. *That* was what was the matter with her. She was a dove. Oh *wasn't* she? — it echoed within her as she became aware of the sound, outside, of the return of their friends.

(19, V, vi, p. 283)

The very next moment Milly finds herself acting out her new role, offering to Maud Lowder's question about whether Densher has returned the answer "most dovelike" (p. 284). That answer is of course technically a lie ("I don't *think*, dear lady, he's here," says Milly, although simply looking at Kate has already convinced her that Densher has indeed come back); but as a lie that graciously protects Kate, it sounds the dovelike note.

Milly consciously chooses to enact Kate's metaphor, and her decision is at once a gesture of self-acceptance and a radical re-creation of that self. For what is literally "the matter" with Milly Theale is not that she is a dove, but that she is dying. And if the unnamed disease that finally kills her is as much a figurative illness as a literal one, it is a figure which is open to a wide range of readings: one might easily argue that Milly dies because she is too passive, too timid, or like Daisy Miller, her Jamesian prototype, too foolishly innocent to survive in the world of the living. But if Milly is indeed a "dove," her death demands to be read in a different spirit — it becomes an act of supreme self-sacrifice, an affirmative gesture of grace and of love. The metaphor transforms Milly's death, bestows on it a significance that Daisy Miller's pathetic collapse never fully achieves. Although Milly's acceptance of Kate's metaphor is characteristically passive, she finally triumphs by inspiring just such a redefinition of what her life and death have meant:

" . . . she died for you then that you might understand her. From that hour you *did*." With which Kate slowly

rose. "And I do now. She did it *for* us." Densher rose to
face her, and she went on with her thought. "I used to call
her, in my stupidity — for want of anything better — a dove.
Well she stretched out her wings, and it was to *that* they
reached. They cover us."

"They cover us," Densher said.

(20, X, vi, pp. 403–4)

Although the dove image originated in Kate's "stupidity" —
her condescending and superficial labeling of the innocent
American girl — the manner of Milly's death compels Kate to
reinterpret her metaphor, to acknowledge in it resonances far
deeper than she had anticipated. Kate admits defeat,
paradoxically, by asserting that she once spoke more truly
than she knew.

But the cost of Milly's power is life itself; only through her
sacrificial death does she fully become both a "princess"
(Susan Stringham's favorite image of her companion) and a
"dove." Unlike Maggie Verver, she does not survive to enjoy
the consequences of her triumph. Nor does she actively invent
new self-images: the princess and the dove are originally
others' metaphors, not her own. And while Maggie defines
herself anew toward the end of *The Golden Bowl* with
metaphors of energetic creation — the dancer, the actress, the
playwright, the images which Milly adopts evoke states of
being, not action. For if Maggie Verver artfully redesigns the
patterns of her life and the lives of those around her, Milly
allows herself to assume the shapes imposed by others' needs.
Indeed her death itself is, in one sense, the supreme example
of her compliant shape-changing. When she "turns her face
to the wall," Milly makes the ultimately passive gesture —
removing herself from the picture altogether, apparently so
that Kate and Densher, united, may form the only figures in
its design. Milly's dying is in this sense the final, most extreme
act of renunciation in James's fiction. But if Milly does not
assume Maggie Verver's outward control over events,
through her death she nonetheless anticipates Maggie's own
artistry in human arrangements.[15] As the closing words of the

novel tell us, Kate and Densher will "never be again as they were." The pattern of their relationship to one another and to Milly has been permanently recomposed.

By adopting Kate's metaphor and making it truth, Milly releases a powerful subterranean force—a pressure which reveals the hidden stresses in the lovers' bond and ends by shattering that bond entirely. In calling Milly a dove, Kate had presumably meant to gloss over the sinister facts about that young American and the uses to which her innocence might be put, and in so doing to turn possible pain to the uses of compliment and social harmony. In *The Wings of the Dove*, as in all the late fiction, such metaphoric speaking has great force: as the impulse magically to transform and redeem human suffering, it tempts us as the mark of the highest civilization. But by the ironic dialectic of James's world, Kate's metaphor finally acts not to conceal tensions but to reveal them. And at the center of that fine civilization, with its elaborate images and carefully preserved taboos, is a superstitious and terrible awe, akin to that felt by the most primitive of men:

> In his search for the origin of the metaphor a psychologist recently discovered to his surprise that one of its roots lies in the spirit of the taboo. There was an age when fear formed the strongest incentive of man, an age ruled by cosmic terror. At that time a compulsion was felt to keep clear of certain realities which, on the other hand, could not be entirely avoided. . . . Since to primitive man a word is somehow identical with the thing it stands for, he finds it impossible to name the awful object on which a taboo has fallen. Such an object has to be alluded to by a word denoting something else and thus appears in speech vicariously and surreptitiously. When a Polynesian, who must not call by name anything belonging to the king, sees the torches lighted in the royal hut, he will say, "The lightning shines in the clouds of heaven." Here again we have metaphorical elusion.[16]

The sophisticated men and women of James's late fiction are ruled by a "cosmic terror" as powerful as any felt

by Ortega's awe-struck Polynesians. Their world is filled with
unnamable facts:

> He [Densher] hadn't only never been near the facts of her
> condition — which counted so as a blessing for him; he
> hadn't only, with all the world, hovered outside an impene-
> trable ring fence, within which there reigned a kind of ex-
> pensive vagueness, made up of smiles and silences and
> beautiful fictions and priceless arrangements, all strained
> to breaking; but he had also, with every one else, as he now
> felt, actively fostered suppressions which were in the direct
> interest of every one's good manner, every one's pity, every
> one's really quite generous ideal. It was a conspiracy of
> silence, as the *cliché* went, to which no one had made an
> exception, the great smudge of mortality across the pic-
> ture, the shadow of pain and horror, finding in no quarter
> a surface of spirit or of speech that consented to reflect it.
> "The mere aesthetic instinct of mankind—!" our young
> man had more than once, in the connexion, said to him-
> self.

(20, IX, iv, pp. 298–99)

In *The Wings of the Dove* "the great smudge of mortality"
hovers continually over events as an unspoken presence, yet
the conspiracy of silence extends far beyond the simple fact of
Milly's impending death. Taboo breeds further taboo: Kate's
intentions toward the dying girl and Densher's deeply
ambivalent feelings about those intentions are matters
equally "impossible to name." Similarly, in both *The Ambassadors* and *The Golden Bowl* a taboo falls most obviously on
the subject of adulterous liaisons, but the fear of naming is
not limited to the fact of illicit sex. James's characters act as if
they shared with Ortega's primitives the belief that "a word is
somehow identical with the thing it stands for," yet unlike
those primitives, their fear is inspired not by sacred objects,
but by the deepest and most complex regions of their own
psyches. And the "beautiful fictions" which that fear gener-
ates are correspondingly intricate; if James's people dwell in
a radically metaphoric world, it is at least in part because
they find the reality of fact and feeling so terrifying.

The elaboration of metaphor in which James's characters delight conveys an impression of tremendous energy—an energy suppressed and diverted, but all the more intense for being thus indirect. Even at its most lighthearted, the extension of metaphor is not simply verbal game-playing, nor is it, as Leavis would have it, "a process of judicial stock-taking."[17] The strain which the reader senses in a Jamesian metaphor has as its deepest source this intense struggle between the pressure of feeling and the need to contain that pressure. If we follow such expanded metaphors with our own fearful fascination, we do so because our intellectual delight in their patterns is matched by an unconscious response to the emotions which those patterns both channel and release. Anxious as he is to avoid confrontation, even Strether is continually betrayed by his metaphors:

> Strether, watching, after his habit, and overscoring with thought, positively had moments of his own in which he found himself sorry for her—occasions on which she affected him as a person seated in a runaway vehicle and turning over the question of a possible jump. *Would* she jump, could she, would *that* be a safe place?—this question, at such instants, sat for him in her lapse into pallor, her tight lips, her conscious eyes. It came back to the main point at issue: would she be, after all, to be squared? He believed on the whole she would jump; yet his alternations on this subject were the more especial stuff of his suspense. One thing remained well before him—a conviction that was in fact to gain sharpness from the impressions of this evening: that if she *should* gather in her skirts, close her eyes and quit the carriage while in motion, he would promptly enough become aware. She would alight from her headlong course more or less directly upon him; it would be appointed to him, unquestionably, to receive her entire weight.
>
> (22, X, i, p. 162)

With this image of a runaway carriage and its terrified occupant, Strether captures the helplessness he imagines Sarah to feel, as she is carried along by the social whirl of

Chad and his Parisian friends. But the suspense felt here is Strether's own; will Sarah decide to repudiate Chad and thus, inevitably, Strether himself? Though Strether begins by feeling sorry for her, he ends by imagining a grotesque scene with himself as comic victim — crushed beneath the full weight of the rather portly Mrs. Pocock. By a kind of emotional syntax, the picture of Sarah in a carriage meditating a jump leads Strether to a vision of the jump performed, and thence to an image of himself as the helpless object jumped upon. Like the runaway carriage, the vehicle of the metaphor seems propelled by an energy of its own — an energy which proves stronger than Strether's conscious reluctance, and which carries him ineluctably toward a vision of the confrontation he so dreads.

If James's characters seek to escape themselves through metaphors, they thus risk eventual defeat — for by a Newtonian emotional law, the fears and desires they so energetically suppress emerge with an equal and opposite force through those very same metaphors. Milly Theale leaves Susan Stringham to face Sir Luke and his medical report alone, but the painful knowledge she tries to avoid catches up with her: "What had been at the top of her mind about it and then been violently pushed down — this quantity was again working up" (19, V, vii, p. 301). In James's world, knowledge does "work up," and the paths it takes are often those of metaphorical elaboration; passion finds its release precisely in that which seems a Jesuitical attempt to dodge the realities of fact and feeling.

In its comic violence, Sarah's wild carriage ride oddly resembles Strether's earlier vision of his own inevitable "smash": [18] "the sense that the situation was running away with him," at once his constant terror and his delight, is here projected onto the unfortunate Mrs. Pocock. Of course the carriages in which James's people actually ride do not go riotously out of control; in the late novels, the surface of human lives is formed of quiet walks about the city, visits paid and received, frequent dinners and endless conversation.

When the Pococks arrive, Strether and Jim share a cab from the station and manage to "take a further turn round before going to the hotel" (22, VIII, ii, p. 84) without the slightest mishap. But though readers often complain that nothing ever "happens" in James's late fiction, metaphorically the novels bristle with daring adventures and melodramatic confrontations.[19] Densher after Milly's death, struggling to choose among painful alternatives, is Densher face to face with "a pair of monsters of whom he might have felt on either cheek the hot breath and the huge eyes" (20, X, iii, pp. 351-52); Kate Croy living at her Aunt Maud's is at once the victim of a siege, trapped in her citadel, and a young kid, trembling before a hungry lioness (19, I, ii, pp. 29-30; II, ii, p. 77); proposing to Charlotte, Adam Verver burns his ships — applies a flaming torch and watches "the fine pink glow ... definitely blazing and crackling" (23, II, vi, pp. 215-21). Expanded metaphor becomes dramatic narrative — an entire small tale of adventure and escape: visiting Chad, the Pococks travel breathlessly down what seems a pleasant passageway, only to find themselves trapped in "a brave blind alley" (22, X, i, p. 160); seated in her "great gilded Venetian chair," Fanny Assingham makes a perilous voyage over "deep waters," while the Colonel watches anxiously on the opposite shore until he hears the reassuring bump of her boat (23, III, x, pp. 364-66).

Fanny's spiritual "paddling" is at once mock-heroic and genuinely so; for all the charming incongruity of Bob's fear lest his firmly seated wife suddenly vanish into the depths of an imaginary lake, we cannot help sharing something of his suspense. Indeed the excitement of even the most playful of these metaphoric adventures is partly a matter of their incongruous origins — of the sharp disparity between the drawing rooms of London or Paris and the hazardous jungles of the imagination. In "A Tragedy of Error" (1864), James's first published story, a man literally drowns at sea; in *Roderick Hudson* (1875), the hero falls to his death in an Alpine storm; but by the late novels such perils have moved inward and become the stuff of metaphor. Elaborating these images, telling themselves stories, James's characters dramatize the human need to make such fictions — to channel intense feeling by giving it narrative form. The invention of metaphor becomes for them a means to escape, even to transcend the limits which their world imposes. And their fictions have both charm and power: in all his many tales of painters and writers, James's people are never so truly images of the artist himself as they thus become in his last novels. But the art that frees may simultaneously betray them: in the imagination of metaphor the desire for escape and the impulse toward uncomfortable discovery are strangely entwined. What excites us most deeply in the end is less the thought of beasts and burning ships than of just such strange entanglements.

4   Talking in James

"Of course what's so awfully unutterable is just what we most notice," observes Nanda Brookenham, the disconcertingly precocious heroine of *The Awkward Age* (9, VIII, i, p. 389). She speaks as a moral critic rather than a literary one, but Nanda's pronouncement about her mother's evasive friends might well stand as a commentary on all late Jamesian fiction.[1] For whenever the characters in James's late novels talk, the "awfully unutterable" makes itself insistently felt, a hidden pressure which the reader feels so intensely just because it is hidden. Adultery, theft, deception, betrayal, even the fact of mortality itself—all go unspoken and unnamed. And for the critic the temptation is strong to make these the crucial subjects of the novels; in proportion as the characters refuse to speak of such things, he longs to do so.

In order to talk sanely about the late fiction, we must indeed make explicit much that James's characters so carefully conceal from one another. Yet any such summary of what has "really" been said—whether in the abridgments made by the reader's memory or in the critic's elaborate exegesis—creates a fictional world radically different from James's own. Translating their alien dialect into his own language, the critic rewrites the novels, makes of them fictions with which he can be both morally and aesthetically more comfortable. But neither talking in James nor reading that talk is a comfortable activity. For while James's characters speak, we must continually shift not only our moral and emotional allegiance, but the very assumptions of our epistemology. To read late Jamesian dialogue is to find ourselves troubled by a host of disturbing questions—questions of motive, of ethical judgment, even of fact itself: What does little Bilham intend when he so cryptically calls Chad's liaison with Madame de Vionnet a "virtuous attachment"? How must we judge a Kate Croy or a Charlotte Stant—or, alternatively, an Adam Verver? What does that opaque little man really "know" at the close of *The Golden Bowl*—and for that matter, what do we? More troubling yet, a close reading of the dialogue suggests that in the world of James's late fiction, such ordinary human questions may finally prove unanswerable. We confront late Jamesian dialogue at the risk of a very special form of literary anxiety.

No sooner have they landed in Europe than all James's Americans, whether early or late, appear to find some sort of talk imperative. Even the relatively taciturn Newman has scarcely arrived in Paris before he acquires—or rather is acquired by—the inevitable confidante: the hero of *The American* is in the classic Jamesian situation—"out of his native element" (iii, p. 28),[2] and the more thoroughly expatriated Mrs. Tristram quickly takes it upon herself to advise him in the ways of "the complex Parisian world" (p. 29). A shallow but worldly woman who interprets Europe for her more innocent compatriot, Mrs. Tristram is an early precursor of Maria Gostrey in *The Ambassadors*, even as Newman himself prefigures Lambert Strether. As his guide to European possibilities, Mrs. Tristram will shortly introduce Newman to that daughter of the Old World, Claire de Cintré, and it is to Mrs. Tristram that he will turn for advice when he is bewildered by the chilling response of Claire's aristocratic family to his proposal of marriage. But Mrs. Tristram, despite the similarity of roles, is no Maria Gostrey, and she and Newman speak a very different language from the later pair:[3]

> "I don't believe," said Mrs. Tristram, "that you are never angry. A man ought to be angry sometimes, and you are neither good enough nor bad enough always to keep your temper."

"I lose it perhaps once in five years."

"The time is coming round, then," said his hostess.
"Before I have known you six months I shall see you in a
fine fury."

"Do you mean to put me into one?"

"I should not be sorry. You take things too coolly. It
exasperates me. And then you are too happy. You have
what must be the most agreeable thing in the world — the
consciousness of having bought your pleasure before-
hand, and paid for it. You have not a day of reckoning
staring you in the face. Your reckonings are over."

"Well, I suppose I am happy," said Newman, meditatively.

"You have been odiously successful."

"Successful in copper," said Newman, "only so-so in
railroads, and a hopeless fizzle in oil."

"It is very disagreeable to know how Americans have
made their money. Now you have the world before you.
You have only to enjoy."

"Oh, I suppose I am very well off," said Newman.
"Only I am tired of having it thrown up at me. Besides,
there are several drawbacks. I am not intellectual."

"One doesn't expect it of you," Mrs. Tristram
answered. Then in a moment: "Besides, you are!"

(iii, pp. 31–32)

Talking with Newman about his character and his social
prospects, Mrs. Tristram helps him, in her limited way, to
understand who he is and to predict the sort of man he may
become. But unlike characters in the later novels, the two
do not collaborate in an act of imaginative interpretation.
Newman and Mrs. Tristram talk to each other in self-
contained verbal structures: with only one exception, they
speak not in sentence fragments, but in complete, short,
declarative sentences whose vocabulary is relatively direct
and concrete ("I should not be sorry"; "Oh, I suppose I am
very well off"). They do not build on one another's formula-
tions: Newman is not inspired to new insights about himself
by Mrs. Tristram's way of putting things. When she an-

nounces that he is "too happy," for example, Mrs. Tristram gives as her reason that Newman's "reckonings"—a word which she stresses by using twice—are over. Strether might well take up her word and explore its implications, but no such linguistic curiosity moves Christopher Newman. Only her general assertion that he is happy claims Newman's attention, and he responds to that assertion in the most straightforward manner (" 'Well, I suppose I am happy,' said Newman, meditatively"), allowing even happiness itself to remain unqualified. Neither echoing nor expanding each other's language, these friends keep their verbal and imaginative distance.

Only once is there an exception: echoing Mrs. Tristram's use of the word "successful," Newman goes on to qualify its meaning—"successful in copper . . . only so-so in railroads, and a hopeless fizzle in oil." Syntactically a fragment, this response marks the only point at which one of the pair develops and completes his companion's assertion. But even here the industrial magnate simply distinguishes among possible sources of capitalistic success, rather than among different senses of the word itself. Newman extends Mrs. Tristram's factual knowledge—not her interpretation of his psychological or ontological state. For such interpretation, we must wait for the characters in James's later fiction to speak.

On his third day in Europe, Strether wanders about Chester, accompanied by his own guide and interpreter, Maria Gostrey, and by his friend Waymarsh. Suddenly Waymarsh breaks from the group and makes a "grim dash" for a jewelry store (21, I, iii, p. 42). As they wait for him to emerge with "some extraordinary purchase" (p. 46), Strether and Maria too take up the question of success. "He has struck for freedom," Strether declares:

> She wondered but she laughed. "Ah what a price to pay! And I was preparing some for him so cheap."
> "No, no," Strether went on, frankly amused now;

"don't call it that: the kind of freedom *you* deal in is dear." Then as to justify himself: "Am I not in *my* way trying it? It's this."

"Being here, you mean, with me?"

"Yes, and talking to you as I do. I've known you a few hours, and I've known *him* all my life; so that if the ease I thus take with you about him isn't magnificent" — and the thought of it held him a moment — "why it's rather base."

"It's magnificent!" said Miss Gostrey to make an end of it. "And you should hear," she added, "the ease I take — and I above all intend to take — with Mr. Waymarsh."

Strether thought. "About *me*? Ah that's no equivalent. The equivalent would be Waymarsh's himself serving me up — his remorseless analysis of me. And he'll never do that" — he was sadly clear. "He'll never remorselessly analyse me." He quite held her with the authority of this. "He'll never say a word to you about me."

She took it in; she did it justice; yet after an instant her reason, her restless irony, disposed of it. "Of course he won't. For what do you take people, that they're able to say words about anything, able remorselessly to analyse? There are not many like you and me. It will be only because he's too stupid."

It stirred in her friend a sceptical echo which was at the same time the protest of the faith of years.

"Waymarsh stupid?"

"Compared with you."

Strether had still his eyes on the jeweller's front, and he waited a moment to answer. "He's a success of a kind that I haven't approached."

"Do you mean he has made money?"

"He makes it — to my belief. And I," said Strether, "though with a back quite as bent, have never made anything. I'm a perfectly equipped failure."

He feared an instant she'd ask him if he meant he was poor; and he was glad she didn't, for he really didn't know to what the truth on this unpleasant point mightn't have prompted her. She only, however, confirmed his assertion.

"Thank goodness you're a failure—it's why I so distinguish you! Anything else to-day is too hideous. Look about you—look at the successes. Would you *be* one, on your honour? Look, moreover," she continued, "at me."

(21, I, iii, pp. 43–44)

Strether has known Maria Gostrey for less than twenty-four hours, but already she and he have become verbal collaborators, joined in the "remorseless analysis" of Waymarsh, Woollett, and Strether himself. Unlike Newman and Mrs. Tristram, this pair often talk in sentence fragments—extending and completing one another's thoughts as if they were not so much separate persons as parts of a single self. When Strether asks, "Am I not in *my* way trying it?" (presumably the kind of freedom in which Miss Gostrey deals), and then declares, rather cryptically, "It's this," Maria offers a tentative phrase to elucidate his obscurity: "Being here, you mean, with me?" Characteristically, the grammatical form of her question prompts the parallel shape of Strether's reply: "Yes, and talking to you as I do." Maria and Strether continually echo and qualify each other's words, as the language which one chooses evokes in turn new insights in the other: "The further she went the further he always saw himself able to follow" (21, I, iii, p. 37).

These two are self-conscious conversationalists: the subject of their talk is talk itself. "Remorseless analysis," Strether implies, means freedom—freedom presumably from the remorse with which Woollett, Massachusetts, is so obsessed, but freedom in a larger sense as well. For to talk like this is to question the meaning of the very words one uses, and to question meaning is finally to question value itself. When Maria labels Waymarsh "stupid," Strether registers his objection: "He's a success of a kind that I haven't approached." But Maria in turn questions what he means by "success": "Do you mean he has made money?" Newman and Mrs. Tristram speak as if the word had only a financial sense, but by asking Strether if Waymarsh's success is to be measured in cash, Maria indirectly calls attention to the possibility of other meanings and other values. And by putting her question so bluntly, she suggests that making money is really but a crude definition of success—a suggestion which she subsequently confirms when proclaiming her delight that Strether is by such definition a failure. Talking to Miss Gostrey, as to all his Parisian friends, Strether learns to acknowledge terms and definitions which do not appear in the limited lexicon of Woollett, Massachusetts. He worries whether such talk is "magnificent" or "base" because he rightly senses that the very foundations of his morality are at stake. As Strether will realize when he discovers the Parisian significance of a "virtuous attachment," to question his terms in this way is to cut himself loose from the moral anchorage of Woollett.

Speaking as Strether and Maria do sounds oddly like thinking out loud—as if the long sentences of private meditation, with their elaborate series of qualifiers and their complex subordination, had here been broken down into their component parts, and divided up between the two speakers. By a process of association at once verbal and emotional, one friend expands, qualifies or completes the assertion of the other, even as the meditations articulate a like process within a single mind. If Maria Gostrey is that "most unmitigated and abandoned of *ficelles*," as James calls her in his Preface (*AN*, p. 322), her abandon is thus not so much moral as ontological: as the "lively extractor" of Strether's "value" and the "distiller" of his "essence" (p. 323), she almost loses her own.

Celebrating his devious use of Miss Gostrey, and declaring that "half the dramatist's art . . . is in the use of *ficelles*," James goes on to confess that Waymarsh is another such novelistic device. He could well have extended the list: little Bilham and Miss Barrace in *The Ambassadors* itself, Susan Stringham in *The Wings of the Dove*, Fanny and Bob Assingham in *The Golden Bowl*, the Bradhams in *The Ivory Tower*—all are figures who might seem to belong "less to my subject than to my treatment of it" (*AN*, p. 322). Indeed the late Jamesian novel threatens to engulf its minor characters in its major ones, to make much of its dialogue seem a peculiarly solipsistic communing of self with self. (Of her husband, Fanny Assingham thinks: "He made her, when they were together, talk, but as if for some other person; who was in fact for the most part herself" [23, III, iii, p. 278].) And *The Ambassadors* especially runs this risk, for as the only late novel wholly confined to a single center of consciousness, it continually threatens to make Strether's inner drama its sole reality.

But having been endowed with a name, a history, and particularly a voice, even a minor novelistic character does not dissolve quite so easily. For James to argue that Maria Gostrey's role in *The Ambassadors* is really that of "an enrolled, a direct, aid to lucidity" (*AN*, p. 322) is for him to be disingenuous about both Maria's power and his own. In her conversations with Strether, Maria does not act purely as the "reader's friend" (p. 322); in fact were we to count on her simply to clear things up, we might well grow as bewildered as Strether himself. Maria imposes interpretations as much as she uncovers truths: when she pronounces Strether's talk with her "magnificent," we can only take her word as assertion, not as fact. Strether worries, and Maria speaks "to make an end of it" — temporarily to silence the voice of his Woollett conscience. Miss Gostrey may help both Strether and the reader to see the truth, but that truth is inseparable from her personal manipulation of it. As James himself boasts later on in the Preface, Maria's connection with Strether has been so "artfully dissimulated" that she "achieves, after a fashion, something of the dignity of a prime idea" (*AN*, pp. 323-24).

When the characters in James's late fiction talk, the reader suffers from a kind of epistemological vertigo, for he is granted no secure position from which to judge the moral or even the factual truth of what is being said. As unmitigated *ficelle* and reader's friend, Maria Gostrey should be

the most disinterested of Jamesian speakers, but we often
sense that she is not—that what she says to Strether is
colored by her fondness for him, her desire that he stay
longer in Paris, her refusal overtly to betray Madame de
Vionnet, even simply by a love of intrigue and the exercise
of her own power.[4] We suspect that she knows, or at least
guesses, much more than she is willing to say: when Strether
reports that little Bilham has declared Chad's attachment
"virtuous," Maria agrees that Bilham's phrase is "the 'word' "
that "would serve," but she pauses before replying, as if
hastily to conceal her reservations. Strether himself feels
that something may be amiss, for ". . . her assurance hadn't
so weighed with him as that before they parted he hadn't
ventured to challenge her sincerity. Didn't she believe the
attachment *was* virtuous?—he had made sure of her again
with the aid of that question" (21, IV, ii, p. 182).

At their next meeting, though, she continues to spar with
him:

> "You don't believe in it!"
> "In what?"
> "In the character of the attachment. In its innocence."
> But she defended herself. "I don't pretend to know
> anything about it. Everything's possible. We must see."
> "See?" he echoed with a groan. "Haven't we seen
> enough?"
> "*I* haven't," she smiled.
> "But do you suppose then little Bilham has lied?"
> "You must find out."
> It made him almost turn pale. "Find out any *more*?"
> He had dropped on a sofa for dismay; but she seemed,
> as she stood over him, to have the last word. "Wasn't
> what you came out for to find out *all*?"
> (21, IV, ii, pp. 188–89)

To say that one doesn't "pretend" to know anything is not
quite to deny knowledge. But Maria refuses to answer
Strether's questions directly, choosing to speak vaguely of
"everything" and "all" rather than of concrete possibilities.

She controls the terms of this dialogue, revealing nothing of her own suspicions, even while she pronounces "the last word" before a pale and weak-kneed Strether. We may suspect her of concealment if not of outright lies, but we have no way to confirm that she even has any suspicions to hide. As readers witnessing this exchange, we are left to float in a world seemingly without solid fact — a world in which "everything's possible," and discourse does not so much reveal our truths as create them.

For the "virtuous attachment" will in time appear an illicit liaison, but little Bilham does not exactly prove a liar. His words have left everything open: what he intended them to mean, how he assumed Strether would take them, what in truth a "virtuous attachment" is. To call Chad's relationship with Marie de Vionnet "virtuous" is to speak that language of enigmatic praise in which late Jamesian characters so inordinately delight, and of which Miss Barrace's everlasting "wonderful" is simply a more lavish specimen. Indeed words like "beautiful," "prodigious," "extraordinary," "splendid," arise so often in Jamesian speech that they seem to constitute a secret code — an esoteric vocabulary understood only by the members of a closed social world.[5] But although James's characters talk as if they shared a common language, theirs is a secret society in which each member has potentially his own secret. Strether and Miss Gostrey speak of the woman responsible for Chad's transformation as "good" — but good in precisely what sense?

> "But I'm not talking," he reasonably explained, "of any mere wretch he may still pick up. I'm talking of some person who in his present situation may have held her own, may really have counted."
> "That's exactly what *I* am!" said Miss Gostrey. But she as quickly made her point. "I thought you thought — or that they think at Woollett — that that's what mere wretches necessarily do. Mere wretches necessarily *don't*!" she declared with spirit. "There must, behind every appearance to the contrary, still be somebody — somebody

who's not a mere wretch, since we accept the miracle.
What else but such a somebody can such a miracle be?"

He took it in. "Because the fact itself *is* the woman?"

"*A* woman. Some woman or other. It's one of the things
that *have* to be."

"But you mean then at least a good one."

"A good woman?" She threw up her arms with a laugh.
"I should call her excellent!"

"Then why does he deny her?"

Miss Gostrey thought a moment. "Because she's too
good to admit! Don't you see," she went on, "how she
accounts for him?"

Strether clearly, more and more, did see; yet it made
him also see other things. "But isn't what we want that he
shall account for *her*?"

"Well, he does. What you have before you is his way.
You must forgive him if it isn't quite outspoken. In
Paris such debts are tacit."

Strether could imagine; but still — ! "Even when the
woman's good?"

Again she laughed out. "Yes, and even when the man
is! There's always a caution in such cases," she more
seriously explained — "for what it may seem to show.
There's nothing that's taken as showing so much here as
sudden unnatural goodness."

"Ah then you're speaking now," Strether said, "of
people who are *not* nice."

"I delight," she replied, "in your classifications. But
do you want me," she asked, "to give you in the matter,
on this ground, the wisest advice I'm capable of? Don't
consider her, don't judge her at all in herself. Consider
her and judge her only in Chad."

(21, IV, ii, pp. 169–70)

Twice Strether speaks of a "good woman" and twice
Maria laughs. But though we sense that his definitions are
not hers, Maria carefully avoids making such differences
explicit. When Strether voices his suspicion that "good"
people in her sense are not necessarily "nice" ones in his
own, Miss Gostrey's only answer is that she "delights" in his

"classifications." In a sense, then, Maria deceives him, for by holding all possible meanings of "good" in suspension, she allows him to assume that Chad's woman will behave sexually and morally as Woollett expects its good women to do. But there are also several senses — sexual, aesthetic, even moral — in which Marie de Vionnet will turn out to be an "excellent" woman indeed, and by speaking of her as such, Miss Gostrey enables Strether to see those qualities to which he might otherwise have been blind. Gloriani's garden party and Strether's first meeting with Chad's mysterious benefactress are yet to come; were Strether to have realized at this point that Marie would not prove a good woman in Woollett's sense, he might never have been able to see her as good in any other. Parisian talk thus educates Strether even as it seems to dissemble, for a sufficiently ambiguous language ensures that no hasty judgments can in fact be made, that all possibilities of vision and feeling must remain open.

The longer Strether stays in Paris, the more he sees and feels, and the more virtue he is able to find in that "virtuous attachment." It is as if Bilham had not so much lied to Strether as recalled him to older and more generous meanings of the word — meanings that "virtue" carried before the eighteenth century made it almost exclusively a synonym for sexual purity.[6] Of course Strether must finally acknowledge that adulterous sexuality does indeed bind Chad and Marie; confronted by the sight of them floating down the river together, he is forced painfully to abandon one cherished definition of a "virtuous attachment." But shocked as he is, Strether does not repudiate his former allegiance. Little Bilham's phrase, he argues, was "but a technical lie — he classed the attachment as virtuous. That was a view for which there was much to be said — and the virtue came out for me hugely. There was of course a great deal of it. I got it full in the face, and I haven't, you see, done with it yet" (22, XII, iii, p. 299). Language creates the conditions under which perception is possible: expecting a virtuous attachment, Strether finds one — though the "great deal" of virtue he has awkwardly gotten "full in the face" is not quite the kind he had originally anticipated. Bilham lies only in the context of Woollett's truth, and by the time Strether might knowledgeably charge his friend with deceit, he has left Woollett's restricted meanings and values far behind him. For Strether, and for us as well, the question of what little Bilham "really" meant by his words remains unanswered: we know only what those words can be made to mean.

If talking in Paris slowly helps to transform Strether's sense of what is real, the effect of that transformation is to keep him temporarily passive — to prevent him from hastily snatching up Chad and returning that prodigal son to the coldly maternal bosom of Mrs. Newsome. Strether comes to Paris with a specific ambassadorial mission; he stays in Paris by not directly fulfilling that mission. But in *The Wings of the Dove* and *The Golden Bowl*, conversation does not so much prevent action as shape the terms in which certain kinds of action will be possible. Until she surreptitiously visits Merton Densher's rooms in Venice, Kate Croy binds herself to her lover most directly with talk: "It had come to be definite between them at a primary stage that, if they could have no other straight way, the realm of thought at least was open to them. They could think whatever they liked about whatever they would — in other words they could say it. Saying it for each other, for each other alone, only of course added to the taste" (19, II, i, p. 65). Talk for the lovers is a form of thinking out loud — and in thus thinking together, they mutually call into being a world which neatly fits the shape of their desires. Typically, it is Kate who takes the lead; she asserts and Densher questions:

> "You accused me just now of saying that Milly's in love with you. Well, if you come to that, I do say it. So there you are. That's the good she'll do us. It makes a basis for her seeing you — so that she'll help us to go on."
>
> Densher stared — she was wondrous all round. "And what sort of a basis does it make for my seeing *her*?"

"Oh I don't mind!" Kate smiled.

"Don't mind my leading her on?"

She put it differently. "Don't mind her leading *you*."

"Well, she won't — so it's nothing not to mind. But how can that 'help,'" he pursued, "with what she knows?"

"What she knows? That needn't prevent."

He wondered. "Prevent her loving us?"

"Prevent her helping you. She's *like* that," Kate Croy explained.

It took indeed some understanding. "Making nothing of the fact that I love another?"

"Making everything," said Kate. "To console you."

"But for what?"

"For not getting your other."

He continued to stare. "But how does she know — ?"

"That you *won't* get her? She doesn't; but on the other hand she doesn't know you will. Meanwhile she sees you baffled, for she knows of Aunt Maud's stand. *That*" — Kate was lucid — "gives her the chance to be nice to you."

(20, VI, ii, pp. 24-25)

Densher has been released from journalistic bondage in America only to feel with renewed force his lack of a convenient place "to 'take' his love" (20, VI, i, p. 5). Discovering that in his absence Milly Theale has become an important figure in Kate's circle, he proposes that he and Kate meet in the future at Milly's. But Kate rejects this idea, turning the conversation instead to the American girl's love for Densher and the uses to which that love might be put. She keeps those uses, however, remarkably vague — speaking of Milly's "helping" them to "go on," but never defining more distinctly what "going on" entails, or how precisely Milly will "help." The sinister motives which in hindsight we might attribute to Kate are nowhere made explicit here; we cannot know if at this point Kate has consciously acknowledged them even to herself.[7] But Densher, as usual, seems uneasy with her explanations: indirectly, his repeated questions ask not only for clarification but for reassurance. And

Kate willingly obliges: when he tentatively extends her assertions in dangerous directions ("Don't mind my leading her on?" "Making nothing of the fact that I love another?"), she "put[s] it differently"—dismissing his scruples by imposing alternate endings on their sentences ("Don't mind her leading *you*"; "Making everything . . . to console you"). By the time their conversation ends and Densher, not to take advantage of Aunt Maud's good will, prepares to leave Lancaster Gate, Kate has succeeded in provisionally silencing his doubts: she dismisses his last question (whether they intend to make Milly believe that Kate actually hates Densher) as a "gross way of putting it," and concludes with "an air of having so put their possibilities before him that questions were idle and doubts perverse" (20, VI, ii, p. 30).

Talking to Densher about the aid Milly can provide, Kate does not so much plan the future as predict it. She speaks in the indicative rather than the imperative mood—not telling Densher how he should act, but pronouncing how Milly in fact will. On the face of it, then, Kate exerts no power; she simply helps Densher to understand their situation. Yet a strange coercion operates beneath the surface of this dialogue, for what Kate asserts will happen is also, we suspect, precisely what she wishes to happen: she very much wants Milly to feel just this sort of consolatory love for Densher. The effect of Kate's words is thus curiously to blur the line between fact and desire and between the explanation of circumstances and the creation of them.[8] For by talking to Densher as if he and Milly will respond in this way to one another, Kate helps bring into being the very situation she predicts. Densher leaves with the assumption that Milly has conveniently fallen in love with him and with the implicit promise to act on that assumption and encourage her love.

Densher thinks of himself as "stupid" in comparison with Kate (20, VI, ii, p. 30), but we may wonder if it is not in the power of her will rather than of her intelligence that she really surpasses him. Though she speaks with a certain irony of Maud Lowder's willfulness, Kate herself is more than a match for her aunt: "The very essence of her . . . is that when she adopts a view she—well, to her own sense, really brings the thing about, fairly terrorises with her view any other, any opposite view, and those, not less, who represent that. I've often thought success comes to her . . . by the spirit in her that dares and defies her idea not to prove the right one" (20, VIII, ii, p. 188). Though the niece has a grace and subtlety her massive aunt lacks, the kinship is unmistakable: possessed by that same defiant spirit, Kate exercises a power over her lover that is, in R. D. Laing's sense, virtually hypnotic.[9]

When Kate says of Milly, "She's *like* that," then, is it the force of a sudden insight that gives emphasis to her words, or is it the determination to impose those words so firmly on Densher's consciousness as to exclude all possible alternatives? Even to ask such a question is to recognize the impossibility of ever arriving at a conclusive answer to the problem it poses: we cannot tell where Kate's real belief about the facts ends and the passionate will to shape and control those facts begins.[10] We feel the power behind her italics, but their origin remains obscure.

Of course Kate carefully avoids saying exactly what Milly *is* like—whether, for example, she is truly in love with Densher, or whether she is just easily exploited. Kate's "explanations" are brilliantly vague; again and again she manages to evade the specific and the possibly sinister, to assert firmly and yet to keep things comfortably ambiguous. She answers Densher's questions without dangerously committing either herself or him: when she announces that Maud Lowder's ignorance of Milly's impending death gains Densher "time," he tries to pin her down—"Time for what?" he asks. "For everything!" she replies. "For anything that may happen." Well may Densher respond with a "strained" smile, "You're cryptic, love!" (20, VIII, iii, p. 223). An accomplished mistress of this peculiarly Jamesian art of conversation, Kate Croy will have her equals only in the heroines of *The Golden Bowl*—in Charlotte Stant and in

Maggie Verver herself. And though Densher's frequent questions voice anxiety and doubt, he simultaneously relies on Kate's ambiguity to ward off conscious pain, even as Strether keeps his own thoughts self-protectively vague so as to avoid facing what he half suspects to be the awful truth. In their strange complicity, Kate and Densher seem in fact like the divided halves of a single self—talking as the discordant parts of Strether or Maggie Verver might talk, if those parts could be imagined as separate persons able to converse with one another.

Kate's words are not merely ambiguous, however: like Strether's Parisians, with their talk of "wonderful" Marie de Vionnet and her "virtuous attachment," Kate speaks a language as affirmative as it is elusive. Milly Theale is "exquisite," "prodigious," "wonderful"; the American heiress, Kate proclaims, has "beauty," and so have her own plans for that heiress's future: "I verily believe I *shall* hate you," she says to Densher, "if you spoil for me the beauty of what I see!" (20, VI, ii, p. 30). But the reader, living in a world whose meanings are comparatively fixed, may find it difficult indeed to adjust his sight to Kate's. Given the nature of her plans and the uses for which she intends her American friend, all this talk of beauty and wonder may finally seem the rankest hypocrisy—and Kate Croy herself one of the most dangerous of Jamesian liars. After all, if Strether is deceived by his Parisian friends, he stands at worst to lose his innocence, his income, and Mrs. Newsome, but in *The Wings of the Dove*, Milly's very will to live is at stake. And the deception apparently kills: when Lord Mark reveals the true relation between Densher and Kate, Milly Theale turns her face to the wall and chooses to die.

In fact it is Densher's sense of their mutual hypocrisy—of the discord between their words and their acts—which in the end drives the wedge between him and Kate. The more he comes to know the American girl, the more restive he grows under Kate's soothing definitions, and at Milly's Venetian party, Densher finally brings things to a crisis. His tension perhaps heightened by the strain of talking to Kate while at the same time there floats before him the vision of a dovelike Milly, "let loose among them in a wonderful white dress" (20, VIII, iii, p. 213), Densher begins to find Kate's language sorely "inconsequent." When Kate characteristically pronounces Milly's desire to live "wonderful" and "beautiful," Densher echoes her words as usual — "It's beautiful indeed" — but "he hated somehow the helplessness of his own note" (p. 220). Before the party is over, he will be able to bear that inconsequence no longer; for the first time Densher will compel Kate — and himself — to speak bluntly of their intentions toward Milly. Kate has just assured him that he can tell Susan Stringham whatever he likes about their relationship, for Susan will never reveal her knowledge to anyone. "*There,* accordingly, is your time," she declares:

> She did at last make him think, and it was fairly as if light broke, though not quite all at once. "You must let me say I *do* see. Time for something in particular that I understand you regard as possible. Time too that, I further understand, is time for you as well."
>
> "Time indeed for me as well." And encouraged visibly by his glow of concentration, she looked at him as through the air she had painfully made clear. Yet she was still on her guard. "Don't think, however, I'll do *all* the work for you. If you want things named you must name them."
>
> He had quite, within the minute, been turning names over; and there was only one, which at last stared at him there dreadful, that properly fitted. "Since she's to die I'm to marry her?"
>
> It struck him even at the moment as fine in her that she met it with no wincing nor mincing. She might for the grace of silence, for favour to their conditions, have only answered him with her eyes. But her lips bravely moved. "To marry her."
>
> "So that when her death has taken place I shall in the natural course have money?"
>
> It was before him enough now, and he had nothing

more to ask; he had only to turn, on the spot, con-
siderably cold with the thought that all along — to his
stupidity, his timidity — it had been, it had been only,
what she meant. Now that he was in possession moreover
she couldn't forbear, strangely enough, to pronounce the
words she hadn't pronounced: they broke through her
controlled and colourless voice as if she should be
ashamed, to the very end, to have flinched. "You'll in the
natural course have money. We shall in the natural
course be free."

"Oh, oh, oh!" Densher softly murmured.

"Yes, yes, yes." But she broke off. "Come to Lady
Wells."

He never budged — there was too much else. "I'm to
propose it then — marriage — on the spot?"

There was no ironic sound he needed to give it; the
more simply he spoke the more he seemed ironic. But
she remained consummately proof. "Oh I can't go into
that with you, and from the moment you don't wash your
hands of me I don't think you ought to ask me. You must
act as you like and as you can."

(20, VIII, iii, pp. 224-26)

The moment is a dramatic one — perhaps nowhere else in
the late James are things named so explicitly. Only words
are exchanged, yet Densher feels a shock of recognition as
powerful as Strether's when he meets his adulterers face to
face. For what Densher must at last confront is the full
consciousness he has so long tried to suppress. And with such
consciousness comes a painful sense of the ironic, of all the
discords which no language, however cryptic, can wholly
mask. From this moment on, Densher finds himself increasingly uncomfortable with Kate's "glib" explanations (20, X,
i, pp. 323, 327). More and more he longs to be "free" with
her (20, X, i, p. 318) — free to speak what he feels without
evasion or ambiguity, to reveal the hidden and to name the
unnamed.

And the reader may well share his longing. In *The Wings
of the Dove*, as in all of late James, the pressure of the

unspoken can become almost unbearably intense. A conversation like that at Milly's party brings much relief, and the reader may turn to it with the grateful sense that now at last he knows exactly where he is. But if we finally choose the terms of such a scene over the elusive language which has preceded it, we do so only at great cost. For to decide that Kate Croy is simply a hypocrite and a liar is to ignore her power as an artist — her power to reshape the world according to the demands of her imagination. By proclaiming Milly's desire to live "wonderful" and "beautiful," Kate suppresses much that is sinister, but she also draws attention to all the wonder and beauty that may indeed be found in Milly's situation. Speaking so strongly of the "beauty" which she sees, Kate almost makes her vision truth.

Kate's pronouncements are seductive. Listening to her talk, the reader — like Densher himself — can find his way of seeing strangely transformed. Milly Theale's desire to live does, after all, fit beautifully into Kate's plans: there is something aesthetically satisfying, even wonderful in fact, about the way in which all the pieces of Kate's design fall so neatly into place. Beyond this, Milly's refusal simply to surrender before the threat of death has itself a certain beauty. Hence insofar as the lovers' plot encourages her desire for life, it too may be called beautiful. For if Milly is irrevocably doomed to die, Kate and Densher have at least granted her the illusion of love — have allowed her to "live," as Strether would say, as long as she is able. And though all this may seem of questionable morality, it is certainly "wonderful": there is much in its brilliant design to excite our awe, if not our unqualified approval. Like the cliché metaphors in which James's characters so often speak, Kate's apparently empty words acquire renewed power. As with little Bilham's "virtuous," we are compelled to rediscover buried meanings — to recognize that we may be moved to awe and wonder, even if we are uncertain whether to praise.

Kate's words have force, then, and we learn nothing that ever directly contradicts them. For the world of James's late novels is one in which there are very few hard facts—a world in which much is possible, and a simple assertion carries immense weight. Never knowing to what literal disease Milly Theale succumbs, we may assume that she dies of betrayal; almost as easily, however, we may choose to believe that what kills Milly in the end is not the lovers' ambiguously kind deception, but Lord Mark's brutal truth. We might in fact go even further, and question how deceptive Kate and Densher finally are—especially since Densher does genuinely fall in love with the American girl. It is a measure of the fluidity of James's world that we find it so difficult to know where we stand, either morally or epistemologically. In such a world, to see Kate Croy's language solely as lies would indeed be a failure of vision.

Kate Croy's actions may seem those of a cynical realist, but her language creates a romantic universe in which incompatible possibilities are reconciled, a universe in which selfish desire and generous impulse are momentarily one. It is an immensely attractive vision, not only for Densher— who wishes with equal intensity to possess Kate, Milly's money, and his own self-respect—but for us as well. If artists, as Sir Philip Sidney feared, may be mistaken for liars, James's late novels almost reverse the equation—and convince us that liars are finally to be taken as artists.

In *The Golden Bowl*, Charlotte Stant and the Prince are such liars and such artists. Choosing to speak only in the noblest terms of their adulterous liaison, they apply "at different times different names to the propriety of their case" (23, III, iv, p. 288), for where their love is concerned, neither impropriety nor evil has a name. Pledging their commitment to one another, Charlotte and Amerigo verbally transform their treachery into its opposite, the undertaking of a sacred trust:

> "I only see how, for so many reasons, we ought to
> stand toward them—and how, to do ourselves justice,
> we do. It represents for us a conscious care—"

"Of every hour, literally," said Charlotte. She could rise to the highest measure of the facts. "And for which we must trust each other — !"

"Oh as we trust the saints in glory. Fortunately," the Prince hastened to add, "we can." With which, as for the full assurance and the pledge it involved, each hand instinctively found the other. "It's all too wonderful."

Firmly and gravely she kept his hand. "It's too beautiful."

And so for a minute they stood together as strongly held and as closely confronted as any hour of their easier past even had seen them. They were silent at first, only facing and faced, only grasping and grasped, only meeting and met. "It's sacred," he said at last.

"It's sacred," she breathed back to him. They vowed it, gave it out and took it in, drawn, by their intensity, more closely together. Then of a sudden, through this tightened circle, as at the issue of a narrow strait into the sea beyond, everything broke up, broke down, gave way, melted and mingled. Their lips sought their lips, their pressure their response and their response their pressure; with a violence that had sighed itself the next moment to the longest and deepest of stillnesses they passionately sealed their pledge.

(23, III, v, pp. 311–12)

Despite the almost comic alacrity with which the lovers fall into one another's arms, there is something genuinely solemn here as well — a fleeting sense that by some extraordinary measure of the facts we are indeed in the presence of the "sacred" and the "beautiful." For a brief moment at least, it is not easy to know the language of mutual self-deception from the terms of a new and oddly moving ethic.

Of course the tensions of this scene are finally too strong for us to put much faith in the lovers' version of their case. The juxtaposition of their exalted language and the gestures which their bodies make almost without their knowledge or control ("each hand instinctively found the other. . . . Their lips sought their lips . . .") ironically calls attention to all that they do not say: their "sacred" pledge is sealed with orgasmic violence. Neither Charlotte nor Amerigo makes any mention of their deep passion for one another, yet nowhere in late James is there a scene whose sexuality is more intensely compelling. Like Densher listening to Kate's evasive pronouncements, we may half want to believe in the lovers' noble language, even while we find their acts and their words peculiarly "inconsequent." But by the end of *The Golden Bowl*, we shall no longer be able so willingly to suspend disbelief; by asking us to see events not through the adulterers' eyes, but through their victim's, the novel's second half will heighten our sense of irony, and make it increasingly difficult for us to see that adultery as in any way sacred or beautiful.

At the close of *The Golden Bowl*, the Prince will have completely transferred his allegiance from Charlotte Stant to Maggie, even as in *The Wings of the Dove*, Densher makes a similar movement from Kate Croy to Milly Theale. And the very structure of each novel seems to demand that the reader's sympathies likewise shift — that we finally place our faith rather in Milly's or Maggie's words than in Kate's or Charlotte's. But the ambivalence which so many readers have felt toward Maggie's final victory — and less intensely, perhaps, toward Milly Theale's — should warn us that questions of truth and morality in these novels are to the very last oddly blurred. If we prefer Maggie's talk to Charlotte's, it is not that Maggie speaks honestly while Charlotte lies, but that Maggie is ultimately the superior artist — that her language makes for the most harmonious and inclusive design her world can sustain. For the full truth in James's late novels is never spoken.

If in *The Wings of the Dove* Kate Croy carefully avoids all mention of Milly Theale's impending death, so too does Milly herself. Those who talk with her — Susan Stringham and Densher in particular — often come dangerously near direct reference, but Milly always "saves" them or "lets them off" by pretending not to understand what they have said.

Overtly to acknowledge her illness would be, as Kate sees, "to bring down the avalanche" (20, VII, iii, p. 141); only by pronouncing things "all right" (20, VII, i, p. 105) can Milly hope to make them so. And in *The Golden Bowl*, Maggie Verver makes an analogous choice: watching Adam, Fanny, Charlotte, and Amerigo at their silent game of bridge, she decides to remain quiet rather than to "sound out their doom in a single sentence, a sentence easy to choose among several of the lurid" (24, V, ii, p. 233). Choosing her words with anguished care, she rejects outraged exclamations for that vague and affirmative language of which Charlotte herself has previously been mistress. In the novel's closing scene, Maggie asks her final question about her rival, and her words—both in what they say and in what they so quietly ignore—match any of Charlotte's own: " 'Isn't she too splendid?' she simply said, offering it to explain and to finish" (24, VI, iii, p. 368).

The Golden Bowl is the only late novel which dares to offer such talk as a finish rather than a beginning: in the person of Maggie Verver, James asks us to go behind the lovers' elegant evasions to the terrible pain they conceal— only to engage us, once again, in a reciprocal process of just such evasion and concealment. Yet in the very novel which takes such risks with our response—the novel in which his dialogue is at its most complex and seemingly perverse— James implicitly acknowledges the potential absurdity of all such talk. In the delightful conversations of Fanny and Bob Assingham, he exaggerates characteristic styles of speaking to the point of self-parody: with that artistic self-consciousness which is itself typical of James, he uses this pointedly named couple as comic reflectors, who simultaneously offer relief from the extreme tensions of the rest of the novel and grotesquely mirror those same tensions. The Assinghams are adepts in the Jamesian art of dialogue, and with their voices James finally both mocks and defends his characters' talk. For through the comic encounters of this strange couple, James incorporates into the world of his novel a most serious attack on that world. And in diverting and eventually repulsing that attack, he offers a defense of his final vision at once comic and intensely moving.

Simply in her physical presence, Fanny Assingham is a comically grotesque exaggeration, with her "flagrant appearance" which "nature itself had overdressed," and which she emphasizes by extravagantly decorated clothing, on the theory that "her only course was to drown, as it was hopeless to try to chasten, the overdressing" (23, I, ii, p. 34). Like the members of Mrs. Brookenham's circle in *The Awkward Age*, Fanny appears to live for "good talk"; in her obsessive and seemingly endless analysis of character and motive, she is the classic Jamesian character carried to a farcical extreme. And the interpretations which she works out are fittingly labyrinthine; "nothing was enough, Mrs. Assingham signified, but that she should develop her thought":

Her husband again for a little smoked in silence.
"What in the world, between them, ever took place?"
"Between Charlotte and the Prince? Why nothing —
except their having to recognise that nothing *could*.
That was their little romance — it was even their little
tragedy."
"But what the deuce did they *do*?"
"Do? They fell in love with each other — but, seeing it
wasn't possible, gave each other up."
"Then where was the romance?"
"Why in their frustration, in their having the courage
to look the facts in the face."
"What facts?" the Colonel went on.
"Well, to begin with, that of their neither of them
having the means to marry. If she had had even a little —
a little, I mean, for two — I believe he would bravely
have done it." After which, as her husband but emitted
an odd vague sound, she corrected herself. "I mean if he
himself had had only a little — or a little more than a
little, a little for a prince. They would have done what
they could" — she did them justice — "if there had been
a way. But there wasn't a way, and Charlotte, quite to

her honour, I consider, understood it. He *had* to have
money—it was a question of life and death. It wouldn't
have been a bit amusing, either, to marry him as a pauper
—I mean leaving him one. That was what she had—as *he*
had—the reason to see."

(23, I, iv, pp. 70-71)

Like the other characters in the late novels, Fanny puzzles
out meaning by playing with the implications of language:
one assertion leads to the next by a kind of verbal logic, as
she expands and qualifies her statements, repeats a former
phrase with new emphasis, or makes comparatively more
explicit the connotations of previous words. The chaste
"why nothing" with which she answers Bob's initial question, for example, she immediately qualifies by a thought
which the words themselves have apparently prompted:
what happened between Charlotte and the Prince was
paradoxically their realization that "nothing" *could* happen. Only by putting it into words does Fanny seem to
discover what she thinks; for her, as for so many late
Jamesian characters, talking becomes a form of thinking
aloud. And as her confederate in this strange process, her
husband becomes virtually a part of herself: "He made her,
when they were together, talk, but as if for some other
person; who was in fact for the most part herself" (23, III,
iii, p. 278). Like Maria Gostrey in *The Ambassadors*,
Colonel Bob acts as "an enrolled, a direct, aid to lucidity"—
though "lucidity," it must be admitted, of a rather obscure
sort. The Colonel's questions repeatedly take up points
which his wife has left unexplained, forcing her to elaborate
still further—or else of course simply to give up, which she
steadfastly refuses to do. Demanding definitions of words
like "romance" and "facts," he thus prompts her to respond
with ever more convoluted arguments: the long and involved paragraph with which she concludes the dialogue
quoted above, for example, is but her partial reply to two
simple words of Bob's—"What facts?"

If the dialogues in James's late novels have often struck

readers as bordering on the absurd, Fanny makes our
laughter irresistible. Her verbal habits comically exaggerate
the already elaborate patterns of the late style — as witness
her multiple repetitions and qualifications of the word
"little": "If she had had even a little — a little, I mean, for
two — I believe he would bravely have done it.... I mean if
he himself had had only a little — or a little more than a
little, a little for a prince." The Colonel's mockery directly
calls our attention to the maniac extravagance of his wife's
talk:

> "All their case wants, at any rate," Bob Assingham
> declared, "is that you should leave it well alone. It's theirs
> now; they've bought it, over the counter, and paid for it.
> It has ceased to be yours."
> "Of which case," she asked, "are you speaking?"
> He smoked a minute: then with a groan: "Lord,
> are there so many?"
> "There's Maggie's and the Prince's, and there's the
> Prince's and Charlotte's."
> "Oh yes; and then," the Colonel scoffed, "there's
> Charlotte's and the Prince's."
> "There's Maggie's and Charlotte's," she went on — "and
> there's also Maggie's and mine. I think too that there's
> Charlotte's and mine. Yes," she mused, "Charlotte's and
> mine is certainly a case. In short, you see, there are
> plenty. But I mean," she said, "to keep my head."
> "Are we to settle them all," he enquired, "to-night?"
>   (23, I, iv, p. 75)

Bob knows of only one case, but the number Fanny can see
is virtually infinite; in this dialogue she takes to ridiculous
lengths the kind of elaboration in which the Jamesian
consciousness delights.

When the Colonel scoffs at his wife by reversing the order
of her previous phrase and suggesting that "Charlotte's and
the Prince's case" is a different entity from "the Prince's and
Charlotte's," he parodies those shifts in word order and
emphasis which can assume such overwhelming importance
in the late style. In fact, with his propensity for "edit [ing]

for their general economy the play of her mind, just as he edited, savingly, with the stump of a pencil, her redundant telegrams" (23, I, iv, p. 67), the Colonel begins to sound like some common-sense critic of the late style who has mistakenly stumbled into a Jamesian world. It is as if William James, that blunt and often literal-minded reader of his brother's novels, had suddenly found himself trapped in marriage with one of Henry's characters. Writing to his brother after the publication of the three late novels, William complained:

> You can't skip a word if you are to get the effect, and 19 out of 20 worthy readers grow intolerant. The method seems perverse: "Say it *out*, for God's sake," they cry, "and have done with it." And so I say now, give us *one* thing in your older directer manner, just to show that, in spite of your paradoxical success in this unheard-of method, you *can* still write according to accepted canons. Give us that interlude; and then continue like the "curiosity of literature" which you have become. For gleams and innuendoes and felicitous verbal insinuations you are unapproachable, but the *core* of literature is solid. Give it to us *once* again![11]

Colonel Bob's impatient plea for directness, "But what the deuce did they *do*?" amusingly anticipates William's frustrated, "Say it *out*, for God's sake . . . and have done with it." The ironic counterpoint between such blunt, concise questions and the intricate labyrinths of Fanny's explanations constantly reminds us of the distance between a world of simple fact and the subtle realm which most Jamesian characters inhabit. After the elaborate convolutions of Fanny's reasoning, the Colonel's bluntness *is* often refreshing: in the gruff military man, we satisfy vicariously some of our own impatient need for translation. But by incorporating this ironic critic into the world of his novel, James encourages our laughter even while he wards off any more serious criticism. For the Colonel's bluff honesty and directness are radically limited: his literal-minded reductionism cannot account for the complexity of thought and feeling which lies beneath the surface of his world—a complexity which Fanny, in her grotesque fashion, at least struggles to articulate.[12] In Henry James's world, facts are never quite as simple—or even as knowable—as Bob Assingham or William James would contend.

If Colonel Bob becomes a parody of the literal-minded critic of James, his wife is in one sense a parody of the artist himself: Fanny, after all, has "made" the marriages which form the basis of the plot, and it is she who explains the complications to which those marriages give rise and predicts the way in which the tangled situation will at last be resolved. In fact it is Fanny's anguished sense of responsibility for the circumstances of the novel which motivates her elaborate explanations; conscious of her own guilt should anything go wrong with the marriages she has made, she needs continually to assure herself that nothing *will* go wrong. Like Kate Croy, Charlotte Stant, and finally Maggie herself, Fanny must thus construct an acceptable interpretation of events—one which avoids any hint of danger or discord. When Bob, like Densher, asks a disruptively explicit question, Fanny, like Kate, chooses to ignore it—"treating it as gross":

> "Why hadn't he [the Prince] heard of her [Maggie] from Charlotte herself?"
>
> "Because she had never spoken of her."
>
> "Is that also," the Colonel enquired, "what she has told you?"
>
> "I'm not speaking," his wife returned, "of what she has told me. That's one thing. I'm speaking of what I know by myself. That's another."
>
> "You feel in other words that she lies to you?" Bob Assingham more sociably asked.
>
> She neglected the question, treating it as gross. "She never so much, at the time, as named Maggie."
>
> (23, I, iv, p. 72)

With their direct allusion to the possibility of Charlotte's lying, the Colonel's "other words" are deeply threatening: Fanny can no more acknowledge that Charlotte lies than that she herself does. In her refusal even to recognize Bob's "gross" suggestion, Fanny exaggeratedly mirrors the Jamesian character's habitual verbal strategy—his struggle to maintain apparent harmony by speaking as if all were indeed harmonious. For her, as for so many of James's men and women, "the overt recognition of danger . . . [is] worse than anything else" (23, III, ii, p. 273).

Talking to her husband thus becomes for Mrs. Assingham a form of "proof"—a means of conclusively "demonstrating," both to him and to herself, that no danger exists. A mistress of Jamesian verbal logic, Fanny works out her theory about the original romance between Charlotte and the Prince until she is able to arrive at a quite satisfactory conclusion: " 'There was no question for me of anybody else when I brought the two others together. More than that, there was no question for *them*. So you see,' she concluded, 'where that puts me.' " And having made this pronouncement, she at last feels safe: "She got up, on the words, very much as if they were the blue daylight towards which, through a darksome tunnel, she had been pushing her way. . . . Yes, it was distinctly as if she had proved what was needing proof, as if the issue of her operation had been almost unexpectedly a success. Old arithmetic had perhaps been fallacious, but the new settled the question" (23, I, iv, p. 76). She gets up "on the words" because for Fanny assertion virtually creates truth—so important has talk become for this quintessentially Jamesian character.

Fanny's "new arithmetic" is scarcely the kind of mathematics to which we and the blunt Colonel are accustomed— but absurd as she is, the flamboyant Mrs. Assingham is finally more at home in the Jamesian world than is her straightforward husband. Writing to his brother William after the latter had decried what he mischievously termed *The Golden Bowl*'s "method of narration by interminable elaboration of suggestive reference,"[13] Henry retorted:

I mean (in response to what you write me of your having read *The Golden B*.) to try to produce some

uncanny form of thing, in fiction, that will gratify you, as
Brother — but let me say, dear William, that I shall greatly
be humiliated if you *do* like it, and thereby lump it, in your
affection, with things, of the current age, that I have
heard you express admiration for and that I would sooner
descend to a dishonoured grave than have written. Still I
will write you your book, on that two-and-two-make-four
system on which all the awful truck that surrounds us is
produced, and *then* descend to my dishonoured
grave. . . . I'm always sorry when I hear of your reading
anything of mine, and always hope you won't — you seem
to me so constitutionally unable to "enjoy" it, and so
condemned to look at it from a point of view remotely
alien to mine in writing it, and to the conditions out of
which, *as* mine, it has inevitably sprung — so that all the
intentions that have been its main reason for being (with
me) appear never to have reached you at all.[14]

Like all James's late fiction, *The Golden Bowl* is not
constructed on "that two-and-two-make-four system": in its
world "the old arithmetic" is indeed "fallacious." For Colonel Bob, as for William James, the ideal is "to say a thing in
one sentence as straight and explicit as it can be made, and
then to drop it forever,"[15] but such speech and the point of
view which it entails are finally "alien" to the vision implicit
in *The Golden Bowl*. "What the deuce did they *do*?"
demands Bob Assingham, but the novel suggests that it may
be impossible to give his question a "straight" and "explicit"
answer. It is as if the novel replied instead: " 'What the
deuce did they *do*?' You can't answer that until you know
what you need — and can bear — to know about it."

Throughout the early sections of *The Golden Bowl*, the
Colonel persistently undermines Fanny's verbal proofs: in
his blunt and literalistic commentary can be heard the voice
of a frustrated William James, asserting with a certain gruff
good humor his utter impatience with the elaborate indirections of his brother's characters. But in a most charming
and even moving transformation, this skeptical ironist is
himself converted to the Jamesian style and the Jamesian

vision: he acquiesces in the assumption of a world almost infinitely subtle and almost infinitely subject to verbal manipulation. For the closer Fanny comes to confronting the fact that Charlotte and the Prince are indeed joined in an adulterous liaison, the more intense grows her guilt and her anguish. And so deeply distressed by his wife's suffering does Bob Assingham become that he finally joins in her struggle to create sustaining fictions. It is after the visit to Matcham—an occasion at which Charlotte and Amerigo make their intrigue rather difficult for poor Fanny to ignore—that this transformation in the Colonel makes itself most felt. Into the Assinghams' conversation there now enters "a suspension of their old custom of divergent discussion, that intercourse by misunderstanding which had grown so clumsy now. This familiar pleasantry seemed to desire to show it could yield on occasion to any clear trouble; though it was also sensibly and just incoherently in the air that no trouble was at present to be vulgarly recognised as clear" (23, III, x, p. 365).

Conscious of his wife's imminent danger, of the risk that she might drown in the "deep waters" of her troubled awareness, the Colonel comes to the rescue by helping to articulate a theory which denies the existence of any threat. He and Fanny have "entered . . . without more words, the region of the understood" (23, III, x, p. 378). Tacitly acknowledging the grave necessity of Fanny's verbal games, Bob now phrases his questions and comments so that they encourage, rather than challenge, the development of her thought:

> "They're wonderful," said Fanny Assingham.
> "Indeed," her husband concurred, "I really think they are."
> "You'd think it still more if you knew. But you don't know—because you don't see. Their situation"—this was what he didn't see—"is too extraordinary."
> " 'Too'—?" He was willing to try.
> "Too extraordinary to be believed, I mean, if one

didn't see. But just that, in a way, is what saves them.
They take it seriously."
       He followed at his own pace. "Their situation?"
       "The incredible side of it. They make it credible."
       "Credible then — you do say — to *you*?"
       She looked at him again for an interval. "They believe
in it themselves. They take it for what it is. And that," she
said, "saves them."

                                        (23, III, x, pp. 367–68)

       "Willing to try" to see things Fanny's way, Bob concurs in
her assertion that Charlotte and the Prince are "wonderful,"
and when he echoes her words questioningly, he speaks not
so much to challenge their validity as to request further
elucidation. Although his questions still border on the
dangerous (as does the last one quoted, with its uncomfortable suggestion that Fanny is deceived), the dominant tone
of the Assinghams' talk has clearly changed. Even the gruff
Colonel has been moved by the precariousness of their
situation to join Fanny's verbal conspiracy — to accept a
world in which Charlotte and the Prince are "saved" by
what they believe or, even more tenuously, by what they can
be said to believe. When Bob sees the "large candid
gathering glittering tears" in his wife's eyes, he decides that
"she must reassure him . . . absolutely in her own way. He'd
adopt it and conform to it as soon as he should be able to
make it out" (23, III, x, p. 371). And when he does "make it
out," when "the basis . . . [has] at last once for all defined
itself," "what was the basis, which Fanny absolutely exacted,
but that Charlotte and the Prince must be saved — so far as
consistently speaking of them as still safe might save them?"
(23, III, x, p. 378). From this moment on, the assertion of
safety becomes a kind of ritual to be repeated whenever
danger threatens: in these dialogues the Colonel resembles
"not a little the artless child who hears his favourite story
told for the twentieth time and enjoys it exactly because he
knows what is next to happen" (24, IV, vii, p. 128). Fanny's
fictions take on at least the consistency of truth.
       If the Assinghams' dialogues act as a comic chorus to *The*

Golden Bowl, theirs is a comedy which is thus converted to the uses of serious drama. In Fanny, James mocks the elaborate evasiveness with which his characters so often speak, even while he dramatizes in moving terms the crucial purposes which such language serves. The voice of William James is permitted to intrude into the world of *The Golden Bowl* and to invite us to laughter at its expense; but though we are allowed our measure of mockery, even the jester is finally silenced and converted. The Assinghams' talk is funny, yet it is also oddly exciting and deeply serious: like the gruff Colonel himself—that most William-like of figures—we are moved even as we laugh. For in the end Fanny struggles to create for herself and the others a sustaining fiction, and it is just such struggles—on the public stage and in the depths of the psyche itself—which are at the very center of the Jamesian drama.

In their serio-comic fashion, then, the Assinghams anticipate the final movement of the novel—Maggie Verver's own effort to save her world by speaking of it as safe. Though like Colonel Bob, we may be disposed at first to question Fanny's soothing fictions, much of the story which she so endlessly tells him in the first half of the novel does in fact come true in the second. Maggie and she *make* it true: with Fanny's assistance, Maggie defines a world in which Amerigo acts with "good faith" (24, IV, ix, p. 173) and "high decency" (24, VI, i, p. 326), Adam Verver is "extraordinary" and "magnificent" (24, IV, ix, p. 175), and the entire situation a "success" (24, VI, i, p. 334). If Fanny is a parody of the Jamesian artist, by the end of *The Golden Bowl* it is Maggie who has assumed control of the situation and learned to practice a far less comic art. As the young Princess grows in stature, Fanny settles into the role of artist's helper—one who "might really have been there at all events, like one of the assistants in the ring at the circus, to keep up the pace of the sleek revolving animal on whose back the lady in short spangled skirts should brilliantly caper and posture" (24, IV, iv, p. 71).

Maggie's assistant is also our own, however: Fanny is a

Jamesian double agent. More nearly "the reader's friend" than Maria Gostrey, for example, she speaks not only to the major characters but about them: in *The Ambassadors* we only hear Maria talking to Strether, but in *The Golden Bowl* we are allowed to listen as the Assinghams privately speculate on the motives and actions of the four central figures. Puzzling out her interpretation of what has happened, Fanny thus indirectly helps the reader to puzzle out his own. But as we soon sense, Mrs. Assingham is even less than Miss Gostrey a disinterested witness: her obsessive curiosity is matched by her passionate fear of knowing too much. Double agent that she is, Fanny at once acts as our guide and intensifies our bewilderment. Nowhere else in the late James are our own epistemological problems so acutely, though so comically, raised.

As artist's assistant, Fanny helps Maggie to construct a saving interpretation of her world — an interpretation which we may be inclined, especially if we are fond of Maggie, to take as truth. But we have no way of verifying our theories: denied access to the minds of Charlotte, Adam, and even the Prince, we are confined in the second half of *The Golden Bowl* to the chambers of Maggie's consciousness and, briefly, of the Assinghams' drawing-room.[16] And at the back of our minds must always reverberate Fanny's announcement that to help Maggie, the Assinghams will have "to lie for her . . . to lie *to* her, up and down, and in and out" (24, IV, vii, pp. 122–23). Maggie loses her innocence to a deep need for the truth, but in the closing portions of the novel she chooses to act only as if certain facts were true; if she is to save her marriage, she cannot fully acknowledge all the pain, cruelty, and deceit which may in turn sustain her own fictions. Despite her intense desire to know, she must also suppress knowledge — even lie both to others and to herself. If Charlotte Stant and Kate Croy are liars who virtually become artists, Maggie Verver is an artist who is thus also a liar.

What Fanny and Bob comically reflect, then, Maggie

makes deadly serious — the need, if one is to survive, of creating one's facts and of choosing to act on one's own fictions. Even the mocking Colonel is compelled at last to recognize this necessity. But in a world in which full consciousness is so intensely valued, the conversion of Colonel Bob has also its terrible cost — for it is ominously like the silencing of that part of the psyche which always questions and doubts, which constantly struggles to bring the private language of the self into accord with the world's full truth. The dialectic of Jamesian talk thus strangely mirrors the tensions within the Jamesian consciousness itself. And to understand those tensions is to begin to see why Maggie Verver — though she triumphs where other Jamesian heroes and heroines fail — remains to the end such an ambiguous heroine.

5   The Difficulty of Ending

Maggie Verver in *The Golden Bowl*

James's last completed novel ends with an embrace. "Close to her, her face kept before him, his hands holding her shoulders, his whole act enclosing her" (24, VI, iii, p. 369), the Prince clasps the Princess, and she buries her head in his breast. It is a rare moment in Jamesian fiction—rare not only in the physical immediacy of the Prince's gesture, but in its conclusiveness. His act is one of literary as well as literal enclosure: embracing his wife, Amerigo brings *The Golden Bowl* to an emphatic finish. Maggie Verver's struggle to save her marriage has reached its fulfillment: "She knew at last really why—and how she had been inspired and guided, how she had been persistently able, how to her soul all the while it had been for the sake of this end" (p. 367). Unlike Isabel Archer in *The Portrait of a Lady*, Maggie does not end her story by fleeing from an embrace to an undefined future. James does not leave the Princess, like his earlier heroine, "*en l'air*,"[1] but in her husband's arms.

No other novel of the major phase comes to so apparently definite or victorious a conclusion. "Then there we are!" says Strether in the last line of *The Ambassadors* (22, XII, v, p. 327); but his desire "not, out of the whole affair, to have got anything for myself" (p. 326) makes "there" a very uncertain location indeed. "To what do you go home?" asks Maria Gostrey twice. "I don't know," Strether can only reply. "There will always be something." Like so many Jamesian novels before it, *The Ambassadors* closes with a gesture of renunciation: we know that Strether is deeply changed, but we are told only what he will *not* do—that he will not stay with Maria in Paris and that he will not marry Mrs. Newsome in America. So too *The Wings of the Dove* concludes with a marriage that will not take place—unless we wish to think of Densher as joined in spiritual union with the memory of a dead girl. The last motion of the novel is a gesture of negation: Kate Croy shakes her head, speaking in words which are the tragic inversion of Strether's final statement: "We shall never be again as we were!" (20, X, vi, p. 405). Like Strether's, her last assertion is remarkably without concrete substance. *The Ambassadors* and *The Wings of the Dove* project undefined futures; in outward form, their resolutions are closer to the unfinished destinies of *The Ivory Tower*—a novel which is quite literally open-ended—than to the substantial reunion of Maggie and her Prince.

But the apparent finality of *The Golden Bowl* is in one sense terribly deceptive. With the possible exception of *The Turn of the Screw*, no Jamesian novel has left its readers themselves more *en l'air:* Maggie's reconciliation with her husband arouses many more unanswered questions than Isabel's return to hers.[2] For Maggie Verver is the first Jamesian innocent who confronts painful knowledge by choosing neither renunciation nor death; determining rather to live and to fight, she implicitly chooses instead the ultimate loss of her own innocence. Unlike Strether—and the long line of Jamesian heroes and heroines from whom he descends—Maggie wants very much to have something for herself "out of the whole affair," and she must risk inflicting pain on others as well as herself to achieve her ends. Struggling at once to understand her private world and to reshape it, Maggie Verver becomes James's strangest heroine: a character who combines Milly Theale's innocence, Densher's passive complicity in evil, and Kate Croy's active need for passion and control. It is a moving but uneasy combination: in this last Jamesian princess, the conflicting motives and desires of the central characters in the late fiction are compressed with an almost unbearable intensity.

The resulting strains threaten to shatter not only the Princess herself, but the very coherence of the novel in which she finally rules.

The new elements in the design are of course Maggie's passion for her husband, her determination to win him back — and, perhaps less obviously, the Prince's apparent willingness to be won. Seven years before *The Golden Bowl*, James had written a novel in which a young girl, just emerging from childhood, makes an oddly similar choice: in her demand that the charming Sir Claude desert Mrs. Beale and run away with her — and in her own readiness equally to sacrifice Mrs. Wix — Maisie Farange is the youthful and quasi-innocent precursor of Maggie Verver. Despite endless talk about Maisie's "moral sense," her wish to be alone with Sir Claude — like Maggie's desire for her husband — seems to have very little to do with that faculty; certainly the tears which she wants to shed as the train to Paris pulls away from the station, leaving herself and Claude behind, "had nothing — no, distinctly nothing — to do with her moral sense" (11, xxxi, p. 354). If Maisie nevertheless remains with the relentlessly moral Mrs. Wix, it is not that she repents her original choice, but that Sir Claude finally shrinks from breaking his tie to Mrs. Beale (like Charlotte Stant, the heroine's stepmother). James does not allow his small heroine to have Sir Claude on her own terms; with his other heroines of the nineties, Fleda Vetch and Nanda Brookenham, Maisie must renounce the man she "loves."[3]

But in *The Golden Bowl* the Prince acquiesces in the betrayal of his mistress: the terms of the sexual equation are radically altered. The conflicting desires of *The Golden Bowl* demand that some sacrifice finally be exacted, and if Maggie is not to renounce her claim on the Prince, then Charlotte must be made to surrender hers. The critical debate over James's last novel usually shapes itself in moral terms — in arguments about whether Maggie's victory represents the triumph of a redemptive love or a "diabolic . . .

geometry of destruction"⁴ — but Maggie Verver finally conquers by what in *Maisie* James calls "something still deeper
than a moral sense" (p. 354). In this obscurely compelling
novel, James is most profoundly concerned not with the
vexed question of morality, but with problems of knowledge, of passion, and of power.

For the reader of *The Golden Bowl*, the peculiar division
in the novel's structure is itself problematic. Despite James's
assertion in the Preface that "the Prince, in the first half of
the book, virtually sees and knows and makes out, virtually
represents to himself everything that concerns us" (*AN*, p.
329), the first volume moves freely through the minds of
Adam Verver, Charlotte, Fanny Assingham, and even,
briefly, of Maggie herself. When the Princess awakens to
consciousness in the novel's second volume, her theories
about the past have thus a special authority: having "gone
behind" each of the members of her strange *menage à
quatre*, we have already half known much of what Maggie
now slowly and agonizingly discovers, and her interpretations have therefore the feel of truth. As she speculates on
the relationship of Charlotte and the Prince, we need not
suspect her of suffering, like the narrator of *The Sacred
Fount*, from an excess of erotic imagination. And because
the processes of her mind clarify much that has previously
been obscure to us, Maggie's experience of discovery becomes ours as well. The novel is not a purely spatial form:
though the two-part structure of *The Golden Bowl* might
suggest that we are meant to sympathize equally with both
"sides" in this passionate battle,⁵ the fact that Maggie's
interpretation is the last — and most comprehensive — inevitably draws us closer to her vision of events. The novel
compels us to identify with Maggie not so much because she
is the most virtuous inhabitant of her world, as because her
knowledge of that world is nearest to our own.

And that knowledge is finally the source of the Princess's
extraordinary power. Maggie triumphs not through moral
purity, but through intelligence; she wins in the end

because she possesses the sort of knowledge which Charlotte, despite all her worldly cleverness, lacks. "Ah for things I mayn't want to know I promise you shall find me stupid," Charlotte warns the Prince at Matcham (23, III, ix, p. 363). Of course in the first half of *The Golden Bowl* it has been Maggie herself who thus unconsciously desired, and achieved, stupidity: indeed at Matcham, "the extraordinary substitute for perception that presided, in the bosom of his wife, at so contented a view of his conduct and course" moves the Prince to "a strange final irritation" (23, III, vi, p. 333). But in the second half of the novel, Maggie becomes painfully conscious of her own abandonment and loss; if it is now Charlotte who has grown stupid, it is because she does not want to acknowledge that Maggie herself has left ignorance far behind. Ironically, therefore, Charlotte fulfills her own prediction of stupidity by failing to imagine her rival's capacity for growth. Speaking to his wife, the Prince delivers the verdict on his former mistress: "She ought to have *known* you. . . . She ought to have understood you better. . . . And she didn't really know you at all" (24, VI, ii, p. 347).

"She's stupid," the Prince finally declares (p. 348), and the structure of *The Golden Bowl* grants the reader no certain knowledge with which to refute that judgment, however harsh it may seem. Only for a brief space of time do we really penetrate Charlotte's consciousness and share directly in her vision of events: at the great diplomatic party, the height of her splendor and her triumph, we are accorded the power of seeing things through "the golden glow with which her intelligence was temporarily bathed" (23, III, i, p. 264). Beginning with her dramatic pause "half way up the 'monumental' staircase" (p. 245), the scene is all Charlotte's own — a demonstration from her point of view of "the *proved* private theory that materials to work with had been all she required and that there were none too precious for her to understand and use" (p. 246). But though we share her sense of triumph, her theory proves dangerously premature: the second half of the novel suggests that in Maggie there has indeed been material too precious for Charlotte's understanding and use. And we cannot know whether Charlotte herself comes to recognize her failure of imagination, for in the second volume of *The Golden Bowl* we are allowed no further access to Charlotte's private theories — proved or otherwise. To the reader, this woman of "exceptional radiance" (p. 264) becomes peculiarly opaque: for all we know, she may have grown quite dull indeed.

But if we are nevertheless reluctant to dismiss Charlotte's splendid intelligence so abruptly, our objections are surprisingly anticipated by Maggie herself. Amerigo's pronouncement draws from his wife a "long wail" of protest:

> "She's stupid," he abruptly opined.
> "O-oh!" Maggie protested in a long wail. It had made him in fact quickly change colour. "What I mean is that she's not, as you pronounce her, unhappy." And he recovered with this all his logic. "Why is she unhappy if she doesn't know?"
> "Doesn't know — ?" She tried to make his logic difficult.
> "Doesn't know that *you* know."
> It came from him in such a way that she was conscious instantly of three or four things to answer. But what she said first was: "Do you think that's all it need take?" And before he could reply, "She knows, she knows!" Maggie proclaimed.
> "Well then what?"
> But she threw back her head, she turned impatiently away from him. "Oh I needn't tell you! She knows enough. Besides," she went on, "she doesn't believe us."
> It made the Prince stare a little. "Ah she asks too much!" That drew however from his wife another moan of objection, which determined in him a judgement. "She won't let you take her for unhappy."
> "Oh I know better than anyone else what she won't let me take her for!"
> "Very well," said Amerigo, "you'll see."
> "I shall see wonders, I know. I've already seen them and

am prepared for them." Maggie recalled — she had memories enough. "It's terrible" — her memories prompted her
to speak. "I see it's *always* terrible for women."

(24, VI, ii, pp. 348-49)

The Prince's "logic" is simple: Charlotte's is the bliss of
ignorance. It is the argument with which Kate and Densher
defended to one another their use of Milly Theale, and it
has been the stance of the Prince and Charlotte herself
toward the Ververs ("'They're extraordinarily happy.' Oh
Charlotte's measure of it was only too full. 'Beatifically'"
[23, III, v, p. 310]). But Maggie cannot so easily dismiss the
possibility that Charlotte suffers. She knows that the other
woman's unhappiness has been the necessary price of her
own reunion with the Prince (p. 346) — that "it's *always*
terrible for women" in a world which permits the existence of desires so passionately and so fatefully in conflict.

And it's always terrible, we might wish to add, for the
reader as well. More fully conscious than any of her
manipulative predecessors, Maggie Verver arouses in us at
once an intenser sympathy and a more profound fear. And
the tensions within Maggie which evoke our own deeply
divided response make here for a dialogue of special im-
penetrability, a conversation whose premises seem continually to shift. Maggie tries, perversely, to make the
Prince's logic "difficult" because she must deal with premises which are emotionally, if not logically, almost irrecon-
cilable: acknowledging another's pain, she must nonetheless
continue to act so as to inflict that pain. Unable to echo the
Prince's complacent assertion of Charlotte's ignorance — as
Kate Croy or Charlotte herself might in a similar circumstance — the Princess proclaims her rival's consciousness:
"She knows, she knows!" But when Amerigo probes further — "Well then what?" — Maggie turns, in a gesture remi-
niscent of Kate Croy, impatiently away: "Oh I needn't tell
you! She knows enough." Maggie prefers to affirm her
husband's other and more limited claim — not that Char-

lotte is actually happy, but that she won't let Maggie take her for unhappy. After those wails of protest and moans of objection, the Princess seems to greet this argument with eager relief: "Oh I know better than anyone else what she won't let me take her for!" Too aware of the possibility of Charlotte's unhappiness simply to assert that it does not exist, the Princess must depend on Charlotte's own power to assert saving fictions—on her mastery of an art much closer to Fanny Assingham's "new arithmetic" than to the Prince's bald logic.

By an emotional law of the excluded middle, Maggie's gain would seem to depend on the fact of Charlotte's loss, but the Princess conquers by a logic which bravely—or brazenly—defies such laws. Though Maggie is privately conscious that her victory has exacted a price, publicly she remains in that long line of Jamesian characters who want, as Charlotte herself says, "everything" (23, III, ix, p. 363): the Princess's very definition of success demands, paradoxically, that even the defeated do not acknowledge failure. Only by granting the others the power to invent their own saving fictions can Maggie herself genuinely triumph. If her verbal coercion is finally more effective than that of her manipulative predecessors, then, it is precisely because she does not always control the terms of the discourse. The Princess conquers by affirming the imaginative autonomy of her victims.

Confronting Charlotte for the last time, Maggie thus allows her to assert—and perhaps to half-believe—that returning to America has been all her own idea. The scene takes place in the arbor at Fawns, where Charlotte has apparently sought refuge from a cool house felt as even more oppressive than the unusual heat of the day. Maggie comes in pursuit, but as she approaches her rival, she pauses—lingering "gravely and in silence" so as to give Charlotte time to choose her fiction: "Whatever she would, whatever she could, was what Maggie wanted—wanting above all to make it as easy for her as the case permitted.

That was not what Charlotte had wanted the other night, but this never mattered—the great thing was to allow her, was to fairly produce in her, the sense of highly choosing" (24, V, v, pp. 309-10). Unlike "the other night"—the scene of that "prodigious kiss" in the drawing-room (24, V, ii, p. 251)—it is now Maggie rather than Charlotte who is physically the pursuer; but in verbal aggression Mrs. Verver remains outwardly supreme:

> "I'm glad to see you alone—there's something I've been wanting to say to you. I'm tired," said Mrs. Verver, "I'm tired—!"
>
> "'Tired'—?" It had dropped, the next thing; it couldn't all come at once; but Maggie had already guessed what it was, and the flush of recognition was in her face.
>
> "Tired of this life—the one we've been leading. You like it, I know, but I've dreamed another dream." She held up her head now; her lighted eyes more triumphantly rested; she was finding, she was following her way. Maggie, by the same influence, sat in sight of it . . . . "I see something else," she went on; "I've an idea that greatly appeals to me—I've had it for a long time. It has come over me that we're wrong. Our real life isn't here."
>
> Maggie held her breath. "'Ours'—?"
>
> "My husband's and mine. I'm not speaking for you."
>
> "Oh!" said Maggie, only praying not to be, not even to appear, stupid.
>
> "I'm speaking for ourselves. I'm speaking," Charlotte brought out, "for *him*."
>
> "I see. For my father."
>
> "For your father. For whom else?" They looked at each other hard now, but Maggie's face took refuge in the intensity of her interest. She was not at all events so stupid as to treat her companion's question as requiring an answer; a discretion that her controlled stillness had after an instant justified. "I must risk your thinking me selfish—for of course you know what it involves. Let me admit it—I *am* selfish. I place my husband first."
>
> "Well," said Maggie smiling and smiling, "since that's where I place mine—!"

"You mean you'll have no quarrel with me? So much the better then; for," Charlotte went on with a higher and higher flight, "my plan's completely formed."

Maggie waited — her glimmer had deepened; her chance somehow was at hand. The only danger was her spoiling it; she felt herself skirting an abyss. "What then, may I ask, *is* your plan?"

It hung fire but ten seconds; it came out sharp. "To take him home — to his real position. And not to wait."

(24, V, v, pp. 313-15)

The Princess consciously adopts the role of *ficelle* in Charlotte's drama: her questions serve to elucidate and extend the other woman's "idea," not to challenge it. "I've dreamed another dream," Charlotte triumphantly asserts, and by taking her verbal cues from her rival, Maggie affirms the force and dignity of that "dream." Though we may suspect that even in her dreams the desire to live with Adam in American City has for Charlotte no reality, we are still half moved to belief by the power of her verbal imagination. Hers is a dream which finally may be only a matter of words, not genuine feeling, but it nonetheless holds out to us a consoling possibility. And it is to this imaginative power in the other woman that the Princess temporarily surrenders. Despite all that has happened, despite even the crucial shift in actual power, this exchange recalls for a moment the old Charlotte Stant — that polyglot mistress of language, that woman in whose very first remark to the Prince ("It's too delightful to be back!") were a tone and attitude "as far removed as need have been from the truth of her situation" (23, I, iii, p. 51). "If she was arranging she could be trusted to arrange," the Prince thinks in those first few moments of reunion; and scenes such as this in the arbor at Fawns lend some truth to what might otherwise seem the terrible complacency of his final pronouncement on the fate of his ex-mistress: "She's making her life. . . . She'll make it" (24, VI, ii, p. 349).

Ironically, it is not Maggie, heiress to American candor,

but the Italian Prince, with his heritage of discreet evasion, who at the last minute expresses a desire for brutal frankness. It is the day of Charlotte's and Adam's departure for America, and Maggie has suggested to her husband that he see Charlotte alone for the last time. Amerigo announces the use he intends to make of such an encounter; he will tell Charlotte the truth—that Maggie does in fact "know" all:

> "I shall tell her I lied to her."
> "Ah no!" she returned.
> "And I shall tell her you did."
> She shook her head again. "Oh still less!"
> With which therefore they stood at difference, he with his head erect and his happy idea perched in its eagerness on his crest. "And how then is she to know?"
> "She isn't to know."
> "She's only still to think *you* don't—?"
> "And therefore that I'm always a fool? She may think," said Maggie, "what she likes."
> "Think it without my protest—?"
> The Princess made a movement. "What business is it of yours?"
> "Isn't it my right to correct her—?"
> Maggie let his question ring—ring long enough for him to hear it himself; only then she took it up. " 'Correct' her—?" and it was her own now that really rang. "Aren't you rather forgetting who she is?" After which, while he quite stared for it, as it was the very first clear majesty he had known her to use, she flung down her book and raised a warning hand. "The carriage. Come!"
> (24, VI, iii, pp. 355–56)

"She isn't to know," says Maggie—but only that morning she has spoken quite differently: "She knows! She knows!" (24, VI, ii, p. 348). Hovering on the edge of a logical contradiction, her assertions leave us quite baffled: we know neither what Charlotte "knows" nor even what Maggie *thinks* she knows. But the resolution, if resolution there finally is, has little to do with logic. Affirming the power of Charlotte's intelligence, the Princess nevertheless knows that only the truth of desire, not of fact, will save both herself and her rival: Charlotte "may think"—indeed must think—"what she likes."

Maggie's logic may seem equivocal, and her refusal to be candid, frightening, but James so arranges the terms of this dispute that the Prince's desire for truth fails to arouse our deepest sympathies. Amerigo's language betrays him: by speaking not of being honest with his former mistress, but of his "right to correct her," he reveals a distressing arrogance. The more attractive we have found Charlotte in the past, the more we are moved to echo Maggie's question: " 'Correct' her—? . . . Aren't you rather forgetting who she is?" The exchange is thus profoundly disturbing, for its terms suggest that to be truthful to Charlotte in one sense is to be false, even cruel, in another. The language of *The Golden Bowl* refuses to grant us a simple conflict between truth and deception; it poses instead another, and far more difficult, choice.

Verbally, then, it is not her former lover who proves Charlotte's final champion, but her rival and her conquerer. "The very first clear majesty" which the Princess uses is paradoxically an affirmation of Charlotte's own regal nature: obeying Maggie's commands, the Prince "received Royalty, bareheaded, therefore, in the persons of Mr. and Mrs. Verver, as it alighted on the pavement" (24, VI, iii, p. 356). Charlotte is "great" (24, VI, iii, p. 364); she is "splendid" (p. 368); she is "incomparable" (p. 363): Maggie allows neither her husband, her father, nor the reader to forget who Charlotte is. The "beautiful" (p. 365) Miss Stant may finally be sacrificed to preserve the Princess's marriage, but Maggie speaks and thinks of that sacrifice almost as if it were a celebration. "They were parting," she thinks of her father and herself, "absolutely on Charlotte's *value*":

>—the value that was filling the room out of which they had stepped as if to give it play, and with which the Prince on his side was perhaps making larger acquaintance. If Maggie had desired at so late an hour some last

conclusive comfortable category to place him in for dismissal, she might have found it here in its all coming back
to his ability to rest upon high values. Somehow, when
all was said, and with the memory of her gifts, her variety,
her power, so much remained of Charlotte's! What
else had she herself meant three minutes before by
speaking of her as great? Great for the world that was
before her — *that* he proposed she should be: she wasn't
to be wasted in the application of his plan. Maggie held to
this then — that she wasn't to be wasted. To let his daughter know it he had sought this brief privacy. What a
blessing accordingly that she could speak her joy in it! His
face meanwhile at all events was turned to her, and as
she met his eyes again her joy went straight. "It's success, father."

(24, VI, iii, pp. 365–66)

All this talk of Charlotte's "value" is not merely glib; if we
feel more than a touch of complacency in the Princess here,
we must also acknowledge "the fact of a felt sincerity in her
words" (p. 363). For Maggie is genuinely able to imagine the
magnificence which the Prince, and we ourselves, have
sensed in Charlotte Stant. In the second volume of *The
Golden Bowl*, we are granted no further access to Charlotte's consciousness, and it is Maggie alone who keeps alive
for us the memory of her rival's splendor. Mrs. Verver
herself must perforce remain silent, but her stepdaughter
sympathetically imagines her unspoken self-defense:

She could thus have translated Mrs. Verver's tap against
the glass, as I have called it, into fifty forms; could perhaps have translated it most into the form of a reminder
that would pierce deep. "You don't know what it is to
have been loved and broken with. You haven't been
broken with, because in *your* relation what can there have
been worth speaking of to break? Ours was everything
a relation could be, filled to the brim with the wine of consciousness; and if it was to have no meaning, no better
meaning than that such a creature as you could breathe
upon it, at your hour, for blight, why was I myself dealt

with all for deception? Why condemned after a couple of
short years to find the golden flame — oh the golden
flame! — a mere handful of black ashes?"

(24, VI, i, pp. 329–30)

"The wine of consciousness," "the golden flame": in the
mind of Maggie Verver, Charlotte's passion finds some of its
most poignant images. When Maggie pronounces Charlotte
"beautiful" and "splendid," then, we know that her words
are not simply polite evasions, for we sense behind them a
true imagination of Charlotte's value.

Drawn by the very brilliance of that "golden flame,"
however, we may also find ourselves echoing Charlotte's
imaginary lament: something magnificent has indeed
turned to ashes. But readers like F. R. Leavis, who deplore
the cruel sacrifice of this "relation filled to the brim with the
wine of consciousness," would do well to recall that at the
very beginning of the affair, Charlotte has revealed the
limits of her own imagination: "I can't put myself into
Maggie's skin — I can't, as I say. It's not my fit — I shouldn't
be able, as I see it, to breathe in it" (23, III, v, p. 311).
Though Maggie comes very near to putting herself in
Charlotte's skin, that lady cannot imagine herself in Maggie's.[6] Seduced by Mrs. Verver's "mastery of the greater
style" (24, VI, iii, p. 368), the modern reader risks forgetting that the golden flame is finally Maggie's image, not
her stepmother's — that by imagining the lovers' "wine of
consciousness," the Princess reveals the vintage of her own.

But attractive as it is, it is also this very power of
sympathetic imagination which makes of Maggie Verver so
ambiguous and disquieting a heroine. While Charlotte
delivers a museum-like lecture to a group of visitors at
Fawns, her voice "high and clear and a little hard" (24, V,
iv, p. 290), we hear through Maggie's "conscious ears" — ears
imaginatively attuned to the unspoken — "the shriek of a
soul in pain" (p. 292). The Princess's eyes fill with tears, yet
the pain with which she so sympathizes is of course the pain
which she herself has in large part caused. And the more

intensely do we share her feeling for Charlotte's anguish, the more uneasy must we grow over Maggie's own acts. For unlike Fleda Vetch, unlike Milly Theale, the Princess does not finally choose to sacrifice herself to the imagined needs of others; her self-abasement is verbal only. Maggie's compassion does not radically alter Charlotte's fate: Maggie weeps, but Maggie wins.

While it is simply not true that, as one recent critic has argued, "nowhere does Maggie recognize the darker side of her behavior,"[7] the Princess's moments of recognition are not necessarily consoling. For the direct link between imaginative sympathy and self-sacrifice — that link so crucial to the moral vision of George Eliot and of the earlier James himself — is in *The Golden Bowl* strangely broken. Maggie Verver is no Maggie Tulliver: though Eliot's Maggie, like James's, implicitly chooses to sacrifice others to the demands of her own passion, in *The Mill on the Floss* full consciousness finally makes such self-indulgence impossible. Allowing herself to be "borne along the tide" with Stephen Guest (*The Mill*, VI, xiii), Maggie Tulliver brings pain to Lucy — Stephen's virtual fiancée — to Philip Wakem, and to her brother Tom. But her surrender to Stephen entails, in Eliot's words, "the partial sleep of thought":[8] it is a surrender to a dream. With Maggie's "waking" (xiv) comes the vivid image of the others' suffering ("could she ever cease to see before her Lucy and Philip, with their murdered trust and hopes?" [p. 413]) and the decision to return to St. Ogg's. In the psychology of *The Mill on the Floss*, full consciousness and conscience are one: a more intense imagination of others, Eliot suggests, would have made Maggie's act of betrayal impossible. "If we — if I had been better, nobler, those claims would have been strongly present within me," Maggie tells Stephen, "I should have felt them pressing on my heart so continually, just as they do now in moments when my conscience is awake — that the opposite feeling would never have grown in me, as it has done: it would have been quenched at once . . ." (p. 417).

But in *The Golden Bowl*, Charlotte's "claim" does not even hypothetically "quench" Maggie's "opposite feeling." On the contrary, only in discovering the fact of the adultery—of Charlotte's claim on the Prince—does Maggie confront the full extent of her own need for him.[9] The Princess awakens at once to the imagination of others and of herself, and her heightened awareness finally leads not to self-denial and renunciation but to a passionate, if hidden, act of self-assertion. In *The Golden Bowl*, full consciousness and conscience overlap, but they do not coincide. And much of the moral disquiet which this novel arouses in us stems from just this uneasy conjunction.

For the moral comfort of its readers at least, there is a sense in which *The Golden Bowl* thus gives us a heroine who knows not too little but too much. If the Princess is so equivocal a heroine, the very intensity of her awareness helps, ironically, to make her so: in the second half of the novel, it is in large part Maggie's own imagination of consequences which keeps before us the possibility of the others' pain—and it is her consciousness of self which makes immediate to us the fact of her own deceit. For unlike Kate and Charlotte, her predecessors in the art of verbal manipulation, Maggie is granted by her creator a private language which sometimes calls her public words directly into question. Kate and Charlotte may prove liars, but even privately they themselves do not acknowledge such a possibility: they seduce us as well as their lovers by the strong conviction with which they assert their interpretations of events. When Charlotte pronounces the Ververs "beatifically" happy (23, III, v, p. 310), we may find the complacency of her remark troubling, but we have no way of being sure that Charlotte does not—consciously at least—believe in the Ververs' beatitude. And Charlotte's apparent faith tempts our own. But when Maggie and her stepmother confront one another in the drawing-room at Fawns, and the Princess herself attests to her blissful state ("You must take it from me that I've never at any moment fancied I could suffer by you. . . . You must take it from me that I've never thought of you but as beautiful, wonderful and good"), we know that Maggie lies — and we know it so clearly because she herself does: "The right, the right — yes, it took this extraordinary form of humbugging, as she had called it, to the end. It was only a question of not by a hair's breadth deflecting into the truth" (24, V, ii, pp. 250-51).

We might wish to protest, of course, that "this extraordinary form of humbugging" is all too ordinary a form of conversation in the world of James's late fiction — that if the Princess of *The Golden Bowl* finally rules with hypocrisy and lies, she has merely learned the appropriate language of her kingdom. After all, it is Charlotte whose verbal dexterity has first attracted us, and in the two crucial dialogues with her stepmother, Maggie may be said simply to match her, evasion for evasion, lie for lie. In the drawing-room at evening, the adulterous Charlotte establishes the fiction of her complete innocence, and Maggie, now grown deeply suspicious, nonetheless responds with a declaration of perfect trust:

> "I'm aware of no point whatever at which I may have failed you," said Charlotte; "nor of any at which I may have failed any one in whom I can suppose you sufficiently interested to care. If I've been guilty of some fault I've committed it all unconsciously, and am only anxious to hear from you honestly about it. But if I've been mistaken as to what I speak of — the difference, more and more marked, as I've thought, in all your manner to me — why obviously so much the better. No form of correction received from you could give me greater satisfaction."
>
> . . . .
> " 'If' you've been mistaken, you say?" — and the Princess but barely faltered. "You *have* been mistaken."
>
> (24, V, ii, pp. 248-49)

And in the garden at noon, Charlotte brazenly pretends that she remains in control of her own fate, while the Princess lies so that the other woman's saving fiction may have the semblance of truth. "I want, strange as it may seem to you," Charlotte declares, "to *keep* the man I've married. And to do so I see I must act":

> "You want to take my father *from* me?"
> The sharp successful almost primitive wail in it made Charlotte turn, and this movement attested for the Princess the felicity of her deceit. Something in her throbbed as it had throbbed the night she stood in the drawing-room and denied that she had suffered. She was ready to lie again if her companion would but give her the opening. Then she should know she had done all.
>
> (24, V, v, pp. 315-16)

While we may feel that the humbugging in these scenes is mutual, that so much of Jamesian conversation is in fact humbugging, only in Maggie Verver does James make this consciousness explicit. We have no direct access to what Charlotte is feeling here: her sudden declaration of love for Adam and American City may be a simple lie, yet it may also represent a glorious self-delusion—a delusion so deeply willed that it has become, in a manner of speaking, the truth. But we cannot escape the fact that in these encounters the Princess is a conscious hypocrite, one who delights in "the felicity of her deceit." Attracted as we are by the "serenities and dignities and decencies" with which Maggie Verver hopes to people her world (24, V, ii, p. 236), we remain uncomfortably aware that Maggie's dignity is in part deception, her serenity a lie.

Yet if the Princess is a heroine who disturbs us by knowing too much, there is another sense, paradoxically, in which her consciousness proves inadequate to the world in which she rules—a sense in which we feel ourselves wanting to know more than she does, and are made uneasy by our desire. At her final parting from her beloved father, Maggie consoles herself with the thought that Adam shares in her celebration of Charlotte's "value": "If Maggie had desired at so late an hour some last conclusive comfortable category to place him in for dismissal, she might have found it here in its all coming back to his ability to rest upon high values. Somehow, when all was said, and with the memory of her gifts, her variety, her power, so much remained of Charlotte's!" (24, VI, iii, p. 365). It is a consolation which we as readers can only take on faith; Maggie may or may not have a "last conclusive comfortable category" in which to place Adam "for dismissal"—even her desire for such a category is at most hypothetical—but our own last terms can be neither so conclusive nor so comfortable. Despite the glimpse into his consciousness which the first half of the novel affords, Adam Verver remains for us essentially a mystery, a man whose "unfathomable heart" (24, V, v, p. 305) may stand as a sign of all that the Princess—and perhaps even James himself—ultimately chooses not to confront.

For all his accumulated millions, the little man may simply be, as Fanny Assingham says, "stupid." "Yet on the other hand," she characteristically adds, "he may be sublime: sublimer even than Maggie herself. He may in fact have already been. But we shall never know" (24, IV, vii, p. 135). Comic as Fanny's habitual self-contradictions may seem, her bewilderment mirrors our own: what Adam Verver really "knows"—of the adultery and betrayal, of the radically flawed structure of his life, of his daughter's own painful awakening—remains to the end profoundly obscure. And we are baffled in part because Maggie wills herself to be; despite Fanny's assertion that "*She'll* know—about her father; everything. Everything" (p. 136), the Princess chooses, only half-consciously, to evade the truth about him. Immediately before her second confrontation with Charlotte, Maggie steps quietly into the nursery to visit the sleeping Principino, and finds her father, "the prime protector of his dreams," installed beside him:

> . . . her father sat there with as little motion—with head thrown back and supported, with eyes apparently closed, with the fine foot that was so apt to betray nervousness at peace upon the other knee, with the unfathomable heart

folded in the constant flawless freshness of the white
waistcoat that could always receive in its armholes the
firm prehensile thumbs. . . . She looked over her fan, the
top of which was pressed against her face, long enough
to wonder if her father really slept or if, aware of her, he
only kept consciously quiet. Did his eyes truly fix her
between lids partly open, and was she to take this—his
forbearance from any question—only as a sign that
everything was left to her? She at all events for a minute
watched his immobility—then, as if once more renewing
her total submission, returned without a sound to her own
quarters.

(24, V, v, pp. 305-6)

Like some oriental deity in western dress, Adam Verver sits
inscrutable. In his mysterious immobility he may, like the
deity, know and understand all—or he may simply have
fallen asleep. Maggie wonders, and then returns to her
rooms in silence; she makes no attempt to determine the
real state of her father's consciousness. She prefers to leave
the enigma of Adam Verver undisturbed, to worship, but
not to question him too closely.

When the little millionaire proposes to return with Charlotte to American City, we may choose to believe that he is
fully conscious of why such exile is necessary, that he has a
"certainty" as strong as Maggie's own about the true state of
affairs (24, V, iii, p. 268). But it is Maggie herself, after all,
who has first given Adam his cue: "You don't claim, I
suppose, that my natural course, once you had set up for
yourself, would have been to ship you back to American
City?" she demands—to which Adam responds, "Do you
know, Mag, what you make me wish when you talk that
way? . . . You regularly make me wish I *had* shipped back
to American City. . . . Do you know that if we *should* ship it
would serve you quite right? . . . And if you say much more
we *will ship*" (24, V, iii, pp. 270-71). Only Adam's eyes—
"the light at the heart of which he couldn't blind"—seem to
Maggie a revelation of some hidden knowledge (p. 268); no
direct words are spoken. "They were avoiding the serious,

standing off anxiously from the real, and they fell again and again, as if to disguise their precaution itself, into the tone of the time that came back to them from their other talk, when they had shared together this same refuge" (p. 257). The innocent Electra bond has been shattered (Maggie confesses that she loves her husband "in the most abysmal and unutterable way of all" [p. 262]), but father and daughter, seated on their old garden bench at Fawns, still adhere to the tone of their incestuously Edenic past. Talking with her father, once her most intimate ally, has become for Maggie an exercise in opacity and evasion little different from talking with Charlotte herself.

For to confront her father directly is a risk which the Princess cannot bear to take: it is as if she feared that knowing the truth about him might paralyze her entirely, might make all action and choice impossible. Rather than dare the knowledge of his bewilderment or pain, she thus chooses to act on the hypothesis that he is "all right" — and that somehow he mysteriously sanctions all she does. Her belief that Adam has his own "idea," an idea which magically redeems her "sacrifice" of him, must attest for us more to the power of Maggie's will than to that of her intelligence. The talk in which Adam's plan is made manifest ends not with explanation, but with vision:

> With which, his glasses still fixed on her, his hands in his pockets, his hat pushed back, his legs a little apart, he seemed to plant or to square himself for a kind of assurance it had occurred to him he might as well treat her to, in default of other things, before they changed their subject. It had the effect for her of a reminder — a reminder of all he was, of all he had done, of all, above and beyond his being her perfect little father, she might take him as representing, take him as having quite eminently, in the eyes of two hemispheres, been capable of, and as therefore wishing, not — was it? — illegitimately, to call her attention to. The "successful" beneficent person, the beautiful bountiful original dauntlessly wilful great citizen, the consummate collector and infallible

high authority he had been and still was — these things
struck her on the spot as making up for him in a wonderful way a character she must take into account in
dealing with him either for pity or for envy. He positively,
under the impression, seemed to loom larger than life for
her. . . . Before she knew it she was lifted aloft by the
consciousness that he was simply a great and deep and
high little man, and that to love him with tenderness was
not to be distinguished a whit from loving him with pride.
It came to her, all strangely, as a sudden, an immense
relief. The sense that he wasn't a failure, and could never
be, purged their predicament of every meanness — made
it as if they had really emerged, in their transmuted
union, to smile almost without pain. It was like a new
confidence, and after another instant she knew even still
better why. Wasn't it because now also, on his side, he
was thinking of her as his daughter, was *trying* her,
during these mute seconds, as the child of his blood? Oh
then if she wasn't with her little conscious passion the
child of any weakness, what was she but strong enough
too? It swelled in her fairly; it raised her higher, higher:
she wasn't in that case a failure either — hadn't been, but
the contrary; his strength was her strength, her pride
was his, and they were decent and competent together.

(24, V, iii, pp. 272–75)

Though the grounds for all this beatitude are at best
obscure, Maggie's response is not a question, but a declaration of faith: "I believe in you more than any one" (p. 275).
With "his inscrutable incalculable energy" (p. 273), Adam
Verver has become for his daughter not only a man to love
and to trust, but a being to worship — and the necessary
ground of her faith in herself.

If the Princess makes of her wealthy father a virtual deity,
though, hers is a leap of faith which few readers of *The
Golden Bowl* have been inspired to follow. Little millionaires make dubious gods — especially little millionaires who
betray a passion for collecting people as well as things.[10]
Father and daughter may part on a recognition of Charlotte's "value," but the Ververs' sense of values seems to take

its measure as much from the gold standard as from a human one:

> "It's all right, eh?"
>
> "Oh my dear — rather!"
>
> He had applied the question to the great fact of the picture, as she had spoken for the picture in reply, but it was as if their words for an instant afterwards symbolised another truth, so that they looked about at everything else to give them this extension. She had passed her arm into his, and the other objects in the room, the other pictures, the sofas, the chairs, the tables, the cabinets, the "important" pieces, supreme in their way, stood out, round them, consciously, for recognition and applause. Their eyes moved together from piece to piece, taking in the whole nobleness — quite as if for him to measure the wisdom of old ideas. The two noble persons seated in conversation and at tea fell thus into the splendid effect and the general harmony: Mrs. Verver and the Prince fairly "placed" themselves, however unwittingly, as high expressions of the kind of human furniture required aesthetically by such a scene. The fusion of their presence with the decorative elements, their contribution to the triumph of selection, was complete and admirable; though to a lingering view, a view more penetrating than the occasion really demanded, they also might have figured as concrete attestations of a rare power of purchase. There was much indeed in the tone in which Adam Verver spoke again, and who shall say where his thought stopped? *"Le compte y est.* You've got some good things."
>
> Maggie met it afresh — "Ah don't they look well?"
>
> (24, VI, iii, pp. 359-60)

In a novel whose central symbol is itself a collector's item, a novel in which the Prince and Charlotte too choose vehicles of gold for the tenor of love, we might almost take the language of this scene as purely emblematic — no more sinister in its implications than Spenser's calling his beloved's breasts "twoo golden apples of vnualewd price."[11]

Even the Ververs' "rare power of purchase," after all, may carry a redemptive as well as an economic force.[12] But as they stand in this room so densely filled with precious objects, a room in which Charlotte and the Prince blur disturbingly into sofas, cabinets, and chairs, the Ververs' triumph may seem not so much a transcendence of the material as a surrender to it. "The note of possession and control"—that note which Maggie hears in her father's voice as he pronounces his last words upon his wife (24, VI, iii, p. 365)—rings ominously in our ears: it is a note more worthy of a Gilbert Osmond than of a beneficent god. Though to Maggie "it was all she might have wished" (p. 365), James's readers have rarely felt themselves equally satisfied.

Adam Verver is at once a moral and an intellectual mystery: the Princess's arbitrary faith is a magnificent affirmation, but the grounds on which it rests remain for us both suspect and obscure. Denied access to the sort of knowledge which would make judgment possible, we become, in our bewilderment, strangely like the Prince himself—a man radically cut off from the terms and values of a familiar world and forced to confront the limits of his powers of translation. "Find out for yourself!" Maggie has challenged him (24, IV, x, p. 203), but about his opaque little father-in-law, the Prince can find out nothing:

> Nothing however had reached him; nothing he could at
> all conveniently reckon with had disengaged itself for him
> even from the announcement, sufficiently sudden, of
> the final secession of their companions. Charlotte was in
> pain, Charlotte was in torment, but he himself had
> given her reason enough for that; and, in respect to
> the rest of the whole matter of her obligation to follow
> her husband, that personage and she, Maggie, had so
> shuffled away every link between consequence and cause
> that the intention remained, like some famous poetic
> line in a dead language, subject to varieties of inter-
> pretation.
>
> (24, VI, ii, pp. 344-45)

Like the baffled Prince, readers of the novel are apt to feel themselves exiles in a world whose language is virtually untranslatable: if the ending of *The Golden Bowl* has indeed remained "like some poetic line in a dead language, subject to varieties of interpretation," it is because in the Ververs, James has so obscured the links between cause and consequence, motive and act, that the full meaning of their final gestures must remain impenetrably ambiguous. For Maggie's is a triumph of that Jamesian logic which conquers by defying the seeming contradictions of language and of fact, which from the intractable conditions of human life verbally wills a harmonious resolution.

When the carriage containing Adam and Charlotte has finally rolled out of sight, and the Principino has been spirited away with the accommodating Miss Bogle, Maggie turns at last to the husband she has won. Dreading lest he shatter the serenity of this moment with a direct confession, she seeks from him instead some echo of her own language, some final acknowledgment of the resolution she has willed:

> "Isn't she too splendid?" she simply said, offering it
> to explain and to finish.
> "Oh splendid!" With which he came over to her.
> "That's our help, you see," she added — to point fur-
> ther her moral.
>
> (24, VI, iii, p. 368)

But the Prince cannot necessarily meet her on the ground she has chosen; he can only acknowledge the limitations of his own vision:

> He tried, too clearly, to please her — to meet her in her
> own way; but with the result only that, close to her,
> her face kept before him, his hands holding her shoul-
> ders, his whole act enclosing her, he presently echoed:
> " 'See'? I see nothing but *you*." And the truth of it had
> with this force after a moment so strangely lighted his
> eyes that as for pity and dread of them she buried her
> own in his breast.
>
> (pp. 368–69)

The Prince speaks here the language of a devoted husband, but his words have an ominous sound. For in this impassioned declaration of love we may also hear a confession of failure — and the sign of an irremediable division between husband and wife. Reunited though they finally are, Prince and Princess do not speak the same language, nor see in the drama they have enacted the same "moral." Maggie offers her verdict on Charlotte "to explain and to finish," but the tension between her question and her husband's response is a reminder of all those tensions which continually hover in the spaces between the novel's words, of all that unease which no talk of Charlotte's splendor can magically dispel. The long-awaited embrace of the Princess and her Prince has the appearance of a comic resolution, but in its "pity and dread" are tragic tones.[13]

And though we as readers necessarily see further than the bewildered Prince, there is a sense in which we share at the end in his problem of vision. Like him, we may find ourselves unable to meet Maggie in her own way, to "see" what she seems to: the Princess's language holds out the promise of harmony restored, a world magically transformed, but a full sense of that harmony continues to elude us. Too much seems suppressed or evaded; too many disturbing questions remain. With its marriages reaffirmed and its couples neatly paired off, the ending of *The Golden Bowl* superficially resembles the closed structure of comedy; but what we really witness here is less a closed fiction than a character struggling to will such a fiction. We are confined so closely to Maggie's point of view in the second half of the novel that we are moved intensely to identify with her, yet we may also find our very confinement stifling. Denied a means of clearly distinguishing the social world of the novel from Maggie's invention of it, we cannot directly confirm or deny her language, cannot simply read the ending of *The Golden Bowl* either as comedy or as irony. Rather, we find ourselves once again curiously like the baffled Prince — able to see clearly, at this end, nothing but Maggie Verver herself.

Indeed, how deeply James's own vision penetrates at the novel's close is a troubling and much vexed question. A recent critic complains that toward the end of *The Golden Bowl* James himself grows "coy": when we are told that "to a lingering view, a view more penetrating than the occasion really demanded," Charlotte and the Prince "also might have figured as concrete attestations of a rare power of purchase" (24, VI, iii, p. 360), it is the novelist, Philip Weinstein argues, who shrinks back from that more penetrating view, who finally refuses to count the cost of Maggie Verver's empire.[14] But that characteristic blurring between novelist and characters which the late style effects makes all such distinctions uncertain at best: is it really James who coyly dodges the issues here, or is it simply the Ververs who thus console themselves? Whatever its source, there is no question but that this tranquil parting depends for its very existence on the avoidance of all lingering looks, all probing questions and doubts. Indeed the occasion only exists by virtue of the careful averting of four pairs of eyes: "To do such an hour justice would have been in some degree to question its grounds—which was why they remained in fine, the four of them, in the upper air, united through the firmest abstention from pressure" (p. 361). Not only Maggie and her father, but Charlotte and the Prince as well, seem to conspire in the fiction that their novelistic lives must have this closed ending: "that strange accepted finality of relation, as from couple to couple, which almost escaped an awkwardness only by not attempting a gloss" (p. 361).

As it dramatizes the superb tranquility of this resolution, the novel nearly seduces us into the belief that all this peace is in fact real; by concluding *The Golden Bowl* with the Princess's victory, James makes the shape of his fictional world coincide closely with the shape his heroine has imposed upon it. There is no novelistic time or space, even if there were psychological possibility, for the Prince to begin in turn to play a doubting Densher to Maggie's triumphant Kate. But if it is to James as novelist that we wish finally to ascribe all this passion for closure, this willful suppression of the open ending, it is also to James as novelist that we must attribute the openness which stubbornly persists, the doubts which make themselves felt in their very negation. Though at times *The Golden Bowl* may seem to hover between ambiguity and mere obscurity, between complexity and deep confusions, it derives its power to haunt us precisely from this tension between the reality which its characters will into being and the irreducible "facts" which never wholly vanish—between our delight in Maggie Verver's triumph and our painful if suppressed awareness of its necessary price. Even those readers who have felt compelled to bring that suppressed awareness to the surface, and to conclude that the cost of Maggie's victory has been too great, are indirectly witness to that haunting power.

And if *The Golden Bowl* reaches its moving conclusion only by seeming to foreclose discussion and suppress disturbing questions, the unfinished *Ivory Tower* may stand as evidence that for James himself the hidden questions characteristically surfaced once again. James's last completed novel may close with the apparent triumph of American "innocence" and American capital, but in *The Ivory Tower* the American struggle for wealth has become an overtly sinister enterprise—an "awful game of grab" (25, I, ii, p. 35). Abel Gaw, the wizened old capitalist who appears "like a ruffled hawk . . . with his beak, which had pecked so many hearts out, visibly sharper than ever" (25, I, i, p. 6) has nothing of Adam Verver's mysterious appeal; even Mr. Betterman, the rich benefactor with the name worthy of Bunyan, has only come to realize on his deathbed the "poison" of his life (25, II, ii, p. 112). In the hero of his novel, a young American who returns to his native land after having lived virtually all his life in Europe, James sends a sensitive and cultivated surrogate on the journey which Adam Verver and Charlotte Stant were about to make at the close of *The Golden Bowl*—and in the Newport of *The*

Ivory Tower, Graham Fielder confronts an American City as disturbing as any the reader may have imagined in store for Charlotte. James himself had returned to America in 1904, only to find his beloved Newport "now blighted with ugly uses," "a mere breeding-ground for white elephants."[15] Even as the buried implications of a metaphor so often emerge in the movement of James's late prose, even as Graham Fielder's own images "find . . . him out, however he might have tried to hide from them" (25, IV, i, pp. 252–53), so the sinister possibilities in all the Ververs' talk of wealth and purchase rise dramatically to the surface of *The Ivory Tower*.

And it is from just those sinister possibilities, "the black and merciless things that are behind the great possessions,"[16] that Fielder shrinks—making the ivory tower both a hiding-place for Gaw's ominous letter and a fit talisman for himself. Refusing to denounce Horton Vint's apparent swindle, willing to sacrifice his newly acquired inheritance, the hero of James's preliminary sketch for the novel more closely resembles the dovelike Milly Theale than the combative Princess of *The Golden Bowl*. Indeed, James's notes project for Graham Fielder no such victory as Maggie's: *The Ivory Tower* was to have concluded, like so many Jamesian novels before it, in renunciation. But *The Ivory Tower* we actually possess ends abruptly in mid-sentence—a novel even more drastically open-ended than any James had intended to write. James abandoned his last novel in August 1914: "With the outbreak of the war," wrote Percy Lubbock, "Henry James found he could no longer work upon a fiction supposed to represent contemporary or recent life."[17] Whatever the conjunction of personal and public history which led to that final broken sentence—and to James's abortive return to the equally unfinished *Sense of the Past*— the sequence of events is peculiarly suggestive. Maggie Verver's victory preserves the civilized forms of her world and the closed shape of her novel, but beneath the surface of these lingering nineteenth-century fictions, imposed at such tremendous cost, we feel an almost unbearable strain. That *The Golden Bowl* was to have been followed by a novel which questioned in turn the very basis of those civilized forms has something of the rhythm of a Jamesian paragraph writ large—its suppressed implications, only faintly adumbrated at first, emerging at last with inexorable force. But that the magnificent if uneasy conclusion of *The Golden Bowl* should in fact have been followed by the broken shape of *The Ivory Tower* and the outbreak of the First World War makes for a more disturbing, though equally compelling metaphor.

Unlike poems, whose existence is so intensely a matter of their language, novels seem to have a reality apart from the words that compose them: reading fiction, we succumb to the illusion that its characters and events have an independent existence to which the words on the page merely point. Rarely is this more dramatically true than in our encounters with the late James, where what is evaded and denied by the words we actually read nonetheless compels our fascinated attention. What the characters refuse to talk about, what they refuse even to think, becomes for us—especially in retrospect—the real substance of James's fiction. But the actual experience of reading the late James is still less emotionally tidy than we usually recall. For even as we are consistently drawn "behind" the words on the page to the narrative they conceal, the words themselves exert on us their own fascinations. Few novels demand more persistently that we translate them, yet few novels feel so relentlessly verbal, even so untranslatable. The melodramatic events we decipher, the social and moral questions those events arouse, are perhaps what remain with us longest, but they do not alone shape our experience as we read. The metaphors which develop out of taboo may move us as deeply as the feelings those metaphors conceal: the fictions Jamesian characters imagine and the fictions they speak have, in the immediacy of our reading, a power of their own. Indeed the more susceptible we are to the reading of any novel—the more we characteristically surrender to the realities that words create—the more emotionally rich, if sometimes disquieting, our reading of the late James must be.

Notes

Chapter 1

1. And at the risk of creating one's own far more rigid characters. Thus Philip Rahv invents his own Prince Amerigo—a charming stereotype, but not the Prince of *The Golden Bowl:* "Here James appears to be unaware that the prince, an idle aristocrat (all ornamental being with no chance of becoming, that is, of growth and transformation) who married Maggie for her money and has little to do except play billiards at his club, is highly unlikely to remain faithful to his American wife, who in any case conveys the unmistakable impression of inveterate frigidity." See "Henry James and His Cult," *New York Review of Books,* 10 February 1972, pp. 18-22.

2. For readings essentially sympathetic to the Ververs, and to Maggie in particular, see Frederick C. Crews, *The Tragedy of Manners: Moral Drama in the Later Novels of Henry James* (New Haven: Yale University Press, 1957), pp. 81-114; Laurence Holland, *The Expense of Vision: Essays on the Craft of Henry James* (Princeton: Princeton University Press, 1964), pp. 331-407; Dorothea Krook, *The Ordeal of Consciousness in Henry James* (1962; rpt. Cambridge: Cambridge University Press, 1967), pp. 232-324; Naomi Lebowitz, *The Imagination of Loving: Henry James's Legacy to the Novel* (Detroit: Wayne State University Press, 1965), pp. 130-42; and Christof Wegelin, *The Image of Europe in Henry James* (Dallas: Southern Methodist University Press, 1958), pp. 122-40. Those more critical of the Ververs include Quentin Anderson, *The Imperial Self: An Essay in American Literary and Cultural History* (New York: Random House, 1971), pp. 166-200; F. R. Leavis, *The Great Tradition* (1948; rpt. London: Penguin, 1972), pp. 184-99; F. O. Matthiessen, *Henry James: The Major Phase* (1944; rpt. New York: Oxford University Press, 1963), pp. 81-104; Sallie Sears, *The Negative Imagination: Form and Perspective in the Novels of Henry James* (Ithaca, N.Y.: Cornell University Press, 1968), pp. 155-222; and Philip Weinstein, *Henry James and the Requirements of the Imagination* (Cambridge, Mass.: Harvard University Press, 1971), pp. 165-94. See also R. P. Blackmur's two Introductions to the novel (New York: Grove Press, 1952 and New York: Dell, 1963) in which he seems to shift from a redemptive to a more ironic reading: if Maggie recalls Dante's Beatrice in the former, she suggests to Blackmur in the latter "the Medusa face of life" (p. 10). Walter Wright in "Maggie Verver: Neither Saint nor Witch," *Nineteenth-Century Fiction* 12 (1957): 59-71, and, more recently, Charles Thomas Samuels in *The Ambiguity of Henry James* (Urbana, Ill.: University of Illinois Press, 1971), pp. 210-26, attempt to mediate the debate.

Criticism of the Ververs very quickly becomes criticism of James himself; see especially Anderson, Leavis, and Weinstein.

3. See John Clair, *The Ironic Dimension in the Fiction of Henry James* (Pittsburgh: Duquesne University Press, 1965), pp. 79-102. But compare Joseph Warren Beach: "To a reader of any sophistication there can be no doubt as to the actual relations subsisting between Charlotte and the Prince." Beach goes on to tell a charming tale about two young women friends in the early 1900's: "They were both of them persons of exceptional intelligence, graduates of one of our best colleges for women, both of them of excellent and well-to-do families, both widely read in world literature. The one of them maintained that the relation between Charlotte and Amerigo was 'guilty,' and the other that it was technically 'innocent' and 'platonic.' Of course I had my own opinion, but I am sure that I tried to hold the balance even between these two admirable friends and blue-stockings." "Not all American readers in the early 1900's were persons of sophistication," Beach concludes, "but the problem he points to is not merely a matter of past history, apparently. See *The Method of Henry James* (1917; rpt. Philadelphia: Albert Saifer, 1954), pp. xci-xcii.

4. All references to *The Portrait of a Lady* are to the Houghton Mifflin edition (Boston: 1882). I have chosen to use this text rather than the revised text which James supplied for the New York Edition in 1908 in order to keep the distinctions between Jamesian styles as clear as possible.

5. Or unless, of course, we are to take these not as Charlotte's terms, but as the narrator's — reading them as his heavily ironic version of what she actually thinks. That James uses the *style indirect libre* rather than the first-person to render his characters' thoughts does make the narrator's presence more strongly felt and does allow him to modulate back and forth between the two voices. But to assume that this is suddenly the narrator alone "speaking" would be to deny the actual effect of the indirect style — its power to suggest the patterns, if not the precise syntax, of a character's own thoughts. For more on the narrator's relation to his own characters, see below.

6. Thereby calling into question, as John Tilford has pointed out, that old critical faith in the Joycean disappearance of James's late narrators — a dogma that is in some disrepute, of course, for Joyce himself as well. See "James the Old Intruder," *Modern Fiction Studies* 4 (1958): 157-64.

7. For a useful account of *le style indirect libre*, see Stephen Ullmann, *Style in the French Novel* (Cambridge: Cambridge University Press, 1957), p. 87. Ullmann points out that a passage in this style has the verb tense that would normally follow a phrase like "he said that," but that it is prefaced neither by such a tag nor by quotation marks. At most, says Ullmann, the context offers some indication that we are meant to take the language as the character's rather than the narrator's. See also Franz K. Stanzel, *Narrative Situations in the Novel: Tom Jones, Moby-Dick, The Ambassadors, Ulysses,* trans. James P. Pusack (Bloomington, Ind.: Indiana University Press, 1971), pp. 92-120, for a suggestive account of the time-relationships such a style establishes in *The Ambassadors*. For a related study, see Derek Oldfield, "The Language of the Novel: The Character of Dorothea," in *Middlemarch: Critical Approaches to the Novel,* ed. Barbara Hardy (London: Athlone Press, 1967), pp. 63-86, especially pp. 81 ff.

8. Peter K. Garrett, *Scene and Symbol from George Eliot to James Joyce: Studies in Changing Fictional Mode* (New Haven: Yale University Press, 1969), p. 107; pp. 141-44.

9. For a less sympathetic view of the narrator's relation to his characters, see Leo Bersani, "The Narrator as Center in *The Wings of the Dove*," *Modern Fiction Studies* 6 (1960): 131-44. Bersani argues that the late style reduces James's characters to "nothing more than allegorical representations of the narrator's internal moral choices" and that "the merging of points of view in the narrative perspective of the novel reflects James's failure to conceive of a meaningful contact with the human community" (p. 144).

10. "Is There a Life after Death?" (1910), in *The James Family*, by F. O. Matthiessen (New York: Knopf, 1948), pp. 609-10.

Chapter 2

1. Phantasms do shade into dreams in James's shorter "supernatural" fiction—most notably in "The Great Good Place" (1900). But George Dane's Brotherhood belongs more to the world of Chaucerian dream-vision than to the sleep of a modern fictional character.

2. After the interruption of her marriage, Jane returns to her room: "My eyes were covered and closed: eddying darkness seemed to swim round me, and reflection came in as black and confused a flow. Self-abandoned, relaxed and effortless, I seemed to have laid me down in the dried-up bed of a great river; I heard a flood loosened in remote mountains, and felt the torrent come." Later: "That night I never thought to sleep: but a slumber fell on me as soon as I lay down in bed"; her dream of the red-room follows. See *Jane Eyre*, ed. Jane Jack and Margaret Smith (1847; rpt. London: Oxford University Press, 1969), II, xi, p. 374, and III, i, p. 407. Jane Eyre is of course one of the most prolific dreamers in nineteenth-century fiction.

3. Although there is much disagreement about exactly what a "stream of consciousness" is, a consensus exists that one is not to be found in James. For general discussions, see Lawrence E. Bowling, "What Is the Stream of Consciousness Technique?" *PMLA* 65 (1950): 333-45; Melvin Friedman, *Stream of Consciousness: A Study in Literary Method* (New Haven: Yale University Press, 1955); and Robert Humphrey, *Stream of Consciousness in the Modern Novel* (Berkeley: University of California Press, 1954). Humphrey distinguishes between the "speech" and "prespeech" levels of consciousness (the latter are "not censored, rationally controlled, or logically ordered"); and because a stream of consciousness must for him include both levels, he omits James from consideration (pp. 2-4). Friedman places James in "the stream of consciousness tradition," but feels that his development was somehow retarded by a devotion to logic and syntax (p. 184). Several Jamesian critics also make passing reference to the absence of the stream of consciousness from his fiction. See, for example, Dorothea Krook, *The Ordeal of Consciousness*, p. 390; Naomi Lebowitz, *The Imagination of Loving*, p. 184; and Sallie Sears, *The Negative Imagination*, p. 21.

4. *The Major Phase*, pp. 22-23.

5. Philip Weinstein also makes use of the superficial resemblance between these

two scenes. See *Henry James and the Requirements of the Imagination*, pp. 168–69.

6. Complaints about the difficulty of "the exasperating style," as one early reviewer called it (*The Nation* 86 [1908]: 11), are of course legion—from William James's lament that his brother's late style was "perverse" ("And so I say now, give us one thing in your straighter directer manner. . . . For gleams and innuendoes and felicitous verbal insinuations you are unapproachable, but the *core* of literature is solid. Give it to us once again!" Letter to Henry James [4 May 1907], in *The Letters of William James*, ed. Henry James [Boston: Atlantic Monthly Press, 1920], II, 278) to the accusations of the modern anti-Jacobites. For responses of James's contemporaries to the late style, see *Henry James: The Critical Heritage*, ed. Roger Gard (New York: Barnes and Noble, 1968). For a recent, rather charming attack on the James who "began to write so badly," see John Halverson, "Late Manner, Major Phase," *Sewanee Review* 79 (1971): 214–31. Halverson finally exonerates James. A more conventional complaint is Arthur Scott's "A Protest against the James Vogue," *College English* 13 (1952): 194–201.

7. S. P. Rosenbaum argues that the substitution of "innumerable and wonderful things" is the one revision in the New York Edition of the novel which is clearly to be deplored. See "Editions and Revisions" in the Norton Critical Edition of *The Ambassadors* (New York: 1964), p. 364. Certainly the earlier line ("He found himself supposing everything") conveys a more powerful sense of shock; inclusive and abrupt, it concludes the paragraph with considerable force. But with the typically ambiguous "wonderful," James makes Strether's discovery something at once shocking and genuinely splendid. And "innumerable things," precisely by being less conclusive than "everything," preserves a sense of open-endedness which is crucial to Strether's development. For Strether to discover "everything" at this point is perhaps more dramatic, but it gives too closed a shape to his story.

8. Jane P. Tompkins notes a similar analogy between the plot of "The Beast in the Jungle" and the characteristic sentence structure of that story. See " 'The Beast in the Jungle': An Analysis of James's Late Style," *Modern Fiction Studies* 16 (1970): 185–91. For more general descriptions of Jamesian syntax, see Richard Bridgman, *The Colloquial Style in America* (New York: Oxford University Press, 1966), pp. 94–106; David Lodge, "Strether by the River," in *The Language of Fiction: Essays in Criticism and Verbal Analysis of the English Novel* (New York: Columbia University Press, 1966), pp. 189–213; R. W. Short, "The Sentence Structure of Henry James," *American Literature* 18 (1946): 71–88; and Ian Watt, "The First Paragraph of *The Ambassadors*: An Explication," *Essays in Criticism* 10 (1960): 250–74. A work which confines itself primarily to linguistic analysis is Seymour Chatman, *The Later Style of Henry James* (Oxford: Blackwell, 1972). I am especially indebted to Lodge's and Watt's perceptive and useful discussions.

9. Compare James's plans for another such recognition scene, the moment in *The Ivory Tower* at which Graham Fielder finally confronts the fact that Horton Vint has betrayed him: "Yes, yes, it seems to come to me that I want the *determination of suspicion* not to come at once; I want it to hang back and wait for a big 'crystallisation,' a falling together of many things, which now takes place, as it were, in Rosanna's presence and under her extraordinary tacit action. . . . It kind of comes over me even that I don't want *any* articulation to *himself* of the 'integrity' question in respect to Horton to have taken place at all—till it very momentarily

takes place all at once in the air, as I say, and on the ground, and in the course, of this present scene. Immensely interesting to have made everything precedent to have consisted but in preparation for this momentousness, so that the whole effect has been gathered there ready to break. . . . The great thing, the great find, I really think, for the moment, is this fact of his having gone to her in a sort of still preserved uncertainty of light that amounts virtually to darkness, and then after a time coming away with the uncertainty dispelled and the remarkable light instead taking its place" ("Notes for *The Ivory Tower*," 25, pp. 345–46). In its tortuous phrasing, the "still preserved uncertainty of light that amounts virtually to darkness" captures precisely that strange form of mental illumination in which James's characters so long persist.

10. Critics have noted the Jamesian propensity to resurrect buried metaphors, but like so many observations about the late style, this one usually goes unexplored; the critic generally confines himself to speaking about the increased "vitality" which this idiosyncrasy imparts to James's prose. See, for example, Austin Warren, "Myth and Dialectic in the Later Novels of Henry James," *Kenyon Review* 5 (1943): 556; or Seymour Chatman, *The Later Style*, pp. 109–12.

11. The ambiguity of *The Turn of the Screw* has of course been ceaselessly debated. For representative collections of essays, see *A Casebook on Henry James's "The Turn of the Screw,"* ed. Gerald Willen (New York: Thomas Y. Crowell, 1960) or the Norton Critical Edition of *The Turn of the Screw*, ed. Robert Kimbrough (New York: 1966).

12. "The Novels of George Eliot," *Atlantic* 18 (October 1866): 485.

Chapter 3

1. Thomas Mann, "Death in Venice" (1911), in *Stories of Three Decades*, trans. H. T. Lowe-Porter (1930; rpt. New York: Knopf, 1941), pp. 380, 427.

2. Others have noted this shift in James's titles. See Alexander Holder-Barrell, *The Development of Imagery and Its Functional Significance in Henry James's Novels* (Basel, Switzerland: Francke Verlag Bern, 1959), p. 148; and Naomi Lebowitz, *The Imagination of Loving*, p. 14.

3. *The Ambassadors*, whose title has a relatively literal meaning but is rich in metaphoric overtones, is something of an exception. But *The Ambassadors* is a borderline case in several senses, as I argue below.

4. *The Great Tradition*, p. 193.

5. Dorothea Krook, *The Ordeal of Consciousness*, p. 391. For a further discussion of the images to which Krook and Leavis object, see below.

6. Robert Gale, *The Caught Image: Figurative Language in the Fiction of Henry James* (Chapel Hill, N.C.: University of North Carolina Press, 1964), pp. 18–21, 59–60. For another study which primarily involves classification by vehicle, see Holder-Barrell, *The Development of Imagery*.

7. Several commentators have remarked in passing on the "metaphysical" quality of James's conceits; the resemblance has been sensed, but its significance unexplored. See especially the early Desmond MacCarthy review, "Mr. Henry James and His Public," *Independent Review* 6 (May 1905): 109; and Austin Warren, "Myth and Dialectic," pp. 556–57.

8.

> If they be two, they are two so
> As stiffe twin compasses are two,
> Thy soule the fixt foot, makes no show
> To move, but doth, if the'other doe.
>
> And though it in the center sit,
> Yet when the other far doth rome,
> It leanes, and hearkens after it,
> And growes erect, as it comes home.
>
> Such wilt thou be to mee, who must
> Like th'other foot, obliquely runne;
> Thy firmnes makes my circle just,
> And makes me end, where I begunne.

For the entire text, see John Donne, *The Elegies and The Songs and Sonnets,* ed. Helen Gardner (Oxford: Oxford University Press, 1965), pp. 63-64.

9. *The Ordeal of Consciousness,* p. 391.

10. Austin Warren has pointed out that James's oriental images usually "betoken the strangeness of that East which is East and hence incommunicable to the West" ("Myth and Dialectic," p. 559). The contrast between this mysterious pagoda and the comparable image of the Palladian Church—Adam Verver's architectural metaphor for the Prince (23, II, i, pp. 135-37)—is revealing. The Church, with its more rational and familiar architecture, conveys Adam's sense of the Prince's value and his slight strangeness, but it does not have the ominous and forbidding mystery of the pagoda.

11. George Eliot, *Middlemarch,* Riverside Edition (1871-72; rpt. Cambridge, Mass., 1956), p. 145.

12. This pattern of labyrinthine imagery in *Middlemarch* has been well discussed by, for example, Barbara Hardy, *The Novels of George Eliot: A Study in Form* (London: Athlone Press, 1959), pp. 220-21, and Mark Schorer, "Method, Metaphor and Mind," in *Middlemarch: Critical Approaches to the Novel,* ed. Barbara Hardy (London: Athlone Press, 1967), p. 20.

13. Barbara Hardy has previously called attention to the resemblance between this image and those in *Middlemarch.* See *The Novels of George Eliot,* p. 222.

14. Frederick Crews notes this distinction between the style of *The Ambassadors* and that of the two later novels (*The Tragedy of Manners,* p. 57). For a perceptive account of the comic tone of *The Ambassadors,* see Ian Watt, "The First Paragraph."

15. Indeed, one could see in Milly's ambiguously willed death signs of that same dangerous selfishness which has made Maggie so equivocal a heroine. A debate from George Eliot's *Daniel Deronda* between the young Jewess, Mirah, and her father, Mordecai, is oddly relevant to Milly's case—though here it is the self-sacrificing heroine who takes the role of skeptical critic:

> "And yet," said Mordecai, rather insistently, "women are specially framed for the love which feels possession in renouncing. . . . Somewhere in the later *Midrash,* I think, is the story of a Jewish maiden who loved a Gentile king so well, that this was what she did: —She entered into prison and changed clothes

with the woman who was beloved by the king, that she might deliver that woman from death by dying in her stead, and leave the king to be happy in his love which was not for her. This is the surpassing love, that loses self in the object of love."

"No, Ezra, no," said Mirah, with low-toned intensity, "that was not it. She wanted the king when she was dead to know what she had done and feel that she was better than the other. It was her strong self, wanting to conquer, that made her die."

Mordecai was silent a little, and then argued —

"That might be, Mirah. But if she acted so, believing the king would never know?"

"You can make the story so in your mind, Ezra, because you are great, and like to fancy the greatest that could be. But I think it was not really like that. The Jewish girl must have had jealousy in her heart, and she wanted somehow to have the first place in the king's mind. That is what she would die for."

"My sister, thou hast read too many plays, where the writers delight in showing the human passions as indwelling demons, unmixed with the relenting and devout elements of the soul. Thou judgest by the plays, and not by thy own heart, which is like our mother's."

Mirah made no answer.

(*Daniel Deronda* [1876; rpt. Baltimore, Md.: Penguin, 1967], VIII, lx, p. 803.)

16. Ortega y Gasset, "Taboo and Metaphor," in *The Dehumanization of Art and Notes on the Novel*, trans. Helene Weyl (1925; rpt. New York: Peter Smith, 1951), pp. 33–34.

17. *The Great Tradition*, p. 193.

18. See above, chapter 2.

19. For a thorough discussion of the imagery of adventure in *The Ambassadors*, see John Paterson, "The Language of 'Adventure' in Henry James," *American Literature* 32 (1960): 291–301.

Chapter 4

1. Compare James's own observation on a scene planned for *The Ivory Tower:* "It is by what he [Graham Fielder] 'says' to the Bradhams and to Rosanna (in the way, that is largely, of *not* saying) that I seem to see my values here as best got. . ." ("Notes for *The Ivory Tower*," 25, p. 380). Those "values" depend, of course, on James's expectation that like Nanda, his readers will "most notice" just "what's so awfully unutterable."

2. All page references to *The American* are to the Signet Edition of the novel, with an afterword by Leon Edel (New York, 1963). This edition is based on the 1879 London text which, according to Edel, is more carefully printed than the original text that appeared in Boston in 1877.

3. When juxtaposed with Maria Gostrey, Mrs. Tristram shows her limitations — both as character and as woman. Trapped in a disappointing marriage, she has developed her ironic tone primarily as a weapon with which to battle her husband, while Maria, less rigidly bound by social place, speaks with something of the irony of the detached social critic. Compared with Miss Gostrey's, Mrs. Tristram's

worldliness seems superficial. The narrator's ironically detached stance toward Mrs. Tristram further diminishes her in our eyes: "She lived in Paris, which she pretended to detest, because it was only in Paris that one could find things to exactly suit one's complexion. Besides, out of Paris it was always more or less of a trouble to get ten-button gloves" (iii, p. 27). *The Ambassadors* treats Maria, like Strether, with a gentler and more sympathetic irony.

4. In 1917 Joseph Warren Beach proposed a distinction between two sorts of Jamesian dialogue — that of "confederates" and that of "antagonists": the dialogue of antagonists is more mysterious and allusive than that of confederates, he argued, because the latter reveals the facts of the story and their meaning, while in the former, participants spar delicately with one another, continually trying to hide as well as to reveal information. (See *The Method of Henry James*, pp. 77-92.) Aware that these categories did not quite work, he modified them in his 1954 Introduction, acknowledging that "sometimes a seeming confederate may be, in effect, a deadly antagonist" (p. lxxix). But the case of Maria Gostrey should prove that all such distinctions immediately break down in practice: she is neither Strether's antagonist, nor simply his confederate, nor the one posing as the other. Were it really possible to label the dialogues in this way, reading the late James would be a much less disturbing experience than it actually is. Beach's attempts suggest how uncomfortable even the best of readers can be with the world which James's late style creates.

5. Several critics have taken it as such, speaking of "in-group game [s]," "social cliques," and "homogeneous, closely-knit social group [s]." See David Lodge, *The Language of Fiction*, p. 197; p. 211; Beach, *The Method of Henry James*, p. lxiv; and Dorothea Krook, *The Ordeal of Consciousness*, p. 151.

6. In his discussion of Richardson's Pamela, forever guarding her technical "virtue" from the sinister designs of Mr. B., Ian Watt argues that "the eighteenth century witnessed a tremendous narrowing of the ethical scale, a redefinition of virtue in primarily sexual terms." See *The Rise of the Novel* (1957; rpt. Berkeley, Calif.: University of California Press, 1967), p. 157.

7. Critics have a dangerous tendency unconsciously to fill in such gaps in our knowledge, and then to talk not about James's novel, but about their own, less disturbing fictions. See, for example, Milton Kornfield: "Kate is intelligent throughout the novel and fully conscious of her motives and intentions" ("Villainy and Responsibility in *The Wings of the Dove*," *Texas Studies in Literature and Language* 14 [1972]: p. 341). Kornfield's desire to assess moral responsibility is apparent in the title of his article; his Kate, guilty of thorough premeditation, is certainly a more satisfying villainess than James's.

8. Sallie Sears writes perceptively about the perfect fit between Kate's needs and Milly's situation. See *The Negative Imagination*, pp. 73-74. But it may be more accurate to say that Kate imagines a world to fit her desires, and that in forcefully imagining such a world she half creates it. In Blackmur's illuminating words, "Kate makes poetic versions of reality, she makes ideals smack of her own needs, and promotes steady action." (See his Introduction to *The Wings of the Dove* [New York: Dell Laurel, 1958], p. 15.) If we try to distinguish clearly between the shape of actual facts and the characters' "poetic versions" of them, the language of the late novels continually defeats us.

9. "One way to get someone to *do* what one wants, is to give an order. To get someone to *be* what one wants him to be ... that is, to get him to embody one's

projections, is another matter. In a hypnotic (or similar) context, one does not tell him what *to be*, but tells him what he is. Such *attributions,* in context, are many times more powerful than orders (or other forms of coercion or persuasion). An instruction need not be defined as an instruction." See R. D. Laing, *The Politics of the Family and Other Essays* (1969; rpt. New York: Vintage, 1972), p. 78.

10. In J. L. Austin's terms, the *force* of her utterances remains ambiguous. Interestingly enough, this very ambiguity in their speech suggests once again that James's sophisticates have a strange kinship with the very primitive. For according to Austin at least, in primitive forms of utterance different forces are not explicitly distinguished; clarification comes only much later in the development of language. See *How to Do Things with Words* (1962; rpt. New York: Oxford University Press, 1970), p. 72; the entire book, indeed, makes a very instructive accompaniment to the reading of late James.

11. William James to Henry James, 4 May 1907, in *The Letters of William James,* II, 278.

12. Whether or not Bob is actually less perceptive than Fanny is open to question, for the Colonel is a very ambiguous figure indeed. At times he appears simply a literal-minded and limited man who is quite baffled by his wife's flights of fancy; but at other moments he seems quite clearly a self-conscious ironist, acutely aware of both the value and the limitations of Fanny's perceptions. We can never know how "stupid" the Colonel actually is, any more than we can ever discover how much Adam Verver really "knows."

13. William James to Henry James, 22 October 1905, in *The Thought and Character of William James,* by Ralph Barton Perry (Boston: Little Brown, 1935), I, 424.

14. Henry James to William James, 23 November 1905, in *The Letters of Henry James,* ed. Percy Lubbock (New York: Scribner's, 1920), II, 43.

15. William James to Henry James, 4 May 1907, in *The Letters of William James,* II, 277.

16. Although her consciousness dominates the second half of *The Golden Bowl,* in one chapter (24, IV, vii) the Princess does not appear at all. Temporarily liberated from the restrictions of Maggie's point of view, we go instead to Cadogan Place and listen to the Assinghams, engaged — as always — in discussing the Ververs.

Chapter 5

1. Henry James, *The Notebooks of Henry James,* ed. F. O. Matthiessen and Kenneth B. Murdock (1947; rpt. New York: George Braziller, 1955), p. 18: "The obvious criticism of course will be that it [*The Portrait of a Lady*] is not finished — that I have not seen the heroine to the end of her situation — that I have left her *en l'air.* — This is both true and false. The *whole* of anything is never told; you can only take what groups together. What I have done has that unity — it groups together. It is complete in itself — and the rest may be taken up or not, later."

2. See chapter 1, note 2, for references to the critical debate surrounding this novel. I owe a particular debt to Philip Weinstein, whose acute chapter on *The Golden Bowl* (*Henry James and the Requirements of the Imagination,* pp. 165-201) has several obvious points of connection with my own. I too am

concerned by much of what troubles him in this novel, though my sense of what is crucial in the reading of it is finally quite different. But even where I disagree with him, I have found his argument stimulating.

3. The sense in which Maisie "loves" Sir Claude—the degree of sexual passion in her feeling for him—remains, like so much else in *What Maisie Knew*, rather ambiguous. Certainly we feel that by the end of the novel Maisie has left her childhood behind her. Accused of destroying her moral sense, Sir Claude responds, ". . . On the contrary, I think I've produced life" (11, xxxi, p. 354).

4. Sallie Sears, *The Negative Imagination*, p. 56; for the argument that Maggie exercises a redemptive love, see, for example, Laurence Holland, *The Expense of Vision*, pp. 377-407; and Dorothea Krook, *The Ordeal of Consciousness*, pp. 232-324, especially pp. 240-79.

5. Sallie Sears argues that the two-part structure of the novel thus divides our sympathy. See *The Negative Imagination*, pp. 173-83.

6. Charles Samuels is also struck by the implications of this passage, and is more just to Maggie here than most recent commentators. See *The Ambiguity of Henry James*, p. 216.

7. Philip Weinstein, *Henry James and the Requirements of the Imagination*, p. 185.

8. George Eliot, *The Mill on the Floss*, Riverside Edition, ed. Gordon Haight (1860; rpt. Boston: Houghton Mifflin, 1961), VI, xiii, p. 410. All subsequent references are to this edition.

9. Of course Charlotte's claims on Amerigo are in no sense as socially legitimate as Lucy's on Stephen Guest. Part of Maggie Verver's strength—as well, perhaps, as the modern reader's distrust of her—comes from the conventional righteousness of her position: she is the married woman recovering her own. But it is not simply the form of her marriage which the Princess struggles to save.

10. Matthiessen's objection may stand as representative: "There is not enough discrimination between Mr. Verver's property and his human acquisitions." See "James and the Plastic Arts," *Kenyon Review* 5 (1943): 546.

11. Those metaphorical apples rest in a silver dish, lavishly placed in turn on "a goodly table of pure yvory." Transformed by his metaphor, Spenser's beloved might make a valuable addition to Mr. Verver's collection. See Sonnet LXXVII ("Was it a dreame, or did I see it playne"), in *The Minor Poems*, II, ed. Charles Grosvenor Osgood and Henry Gibbons Lotspeich (Baltimore: Johns Hopkins Press, 1947), p. 227.

12. See Dorothea Krook, *The Ordeal of Consciousness*, p. 322. Her two chapters on *The Golden Bowl* constitute a very thorough account of the ambiguities surrounding Adam Verver and his daughter's triumph.

13. Several critics have touched on the suggestion of tragedy in these final lines. See especially R. P. Blackmur's Introduction to the Dell Laurel *Golden Bowl* (New York: 1963), pp. 5-13; and Dorothea Krook's response to Blackmur in *The Ordeal of Consciousness*, pp. 317-24.

14. *Henry James and the Requirements of the Imagination*, p. 194.

15. *The American Scene* (1907; rpt. Bloomington, Ind.: Indiana University Press, 1968), pp. 223-24.

16. Henry James, "Notes for *The Ivory Tower*," 25, p. 295.

17. Preface to *The Ivory Tower*, 25, p. v.

Index

Novels and other literary works are indexed under the name of the author; modern critics are represented only by their own names and not by the titles of their works. References from the notes have also been indexed whenever they go beyond mere documentation.